P — Preview
Q — QUESTION
R — ReaD
S — State it in
T — TeST your

PRINCIPLES OF WHEEL ALINEMENT

ReaD CHAPTER #1 Page 12. Review QUIZ.
      CHAPTER #5 Page 60. Review Quize
      CHAPTER #9 Page 96 Review Quize

2⁵⁰

PRINCIPLES OF WHEEL ALINEMENT SERVICE

E. Miles Bacon, M.A.
Director of Training
Bear Manufacturing Company

McGRAW-HILL BOOK COMPANY
New York   St. Louis   San Francisco   Düsseldorf
Johannesburg   Kuala Lumpur   London   Mexico   Montreal
New Delhi   Panama   Rio de Janeiro   Singapore   Sydney   Toronto

CONTENTS

PREFACE

The *Principles of Wheel Alinement Service* is written for the student of wheel alinement, the wheel alinement specialist, and the automotive businessman alike. Its content is organized about the automobile itself as it first enters the door of a Service Center for service. It covers preparatory steps for alinement, wheel alinement fundamentals, adjustments through job completion, and trouble shooting.

The *Principles of Wheel Alinement Service* is an effort to present wheel alinement as it truly is, a complete steering and suspension service. It is a service beyond that of adjusting caster, camber, and toe-in angles to correct tire-wear problems or to make tires last longer. As a complete service, it includes front end parts replacements (ball joints, tie rod ends, relay rods, idler arms, shock absorbers, etc.); it includes wheel balancing services; it includes steering gear adjustments and power steering services and it includes wheel bearing services. So, rather than wheel alinement being an "adjustment" service only, as so popularly regarded, it actually involves servicing the complete automotive steering and suspension system.

The pages of this text express the complete service approach.

E. Miles Bacon

ACKNOWLEDGMENTS

The author wishes to acknowledge and express his appreciation to the following companies which supplied artwork and information used in this book. Without this help and assistance, the authenticity, accuracy, and completeness of the subject area would not have been possible.

Bada Company
Bear Manufacturing Company
Buick Motor Division of General Motors Corporation
Cadillac Motor Car Division of General Motors Corporation
Chevrolet Motor Division of General Motors Corporation
Chrysler-Plymouth Division of Chrysler Corporation
Hunter Engineering Company
D. R. Light Company
J. C. Penney Company, Inc.
Sears, Roebuck and Company
Stewart Warner Alemite Division

Chapter 1
FRONT SUSPENSION DESIGNS

Every good Wheel Alinement Specialist must be thoroughly acquainted with the various kinds of front suspensions that are in current use, their construction, and their operating characteristics. Technical knowledge provides the basis for an intelligent approach to the diagnosis required in problems of wheel alinement and to the methods of repair. Technical knowledge, also, makes the difference between the professional and the so-called "shade-tree" approach to wheel alinement services.

CONVENTIONAL AXLE FRONT SUSPENSION

One of the first automotive front suspensions used is still popular today for trucks, the conventional axle or straight axle design. It consists of an I beam extending approximately the full width of the vehicle. Strong in construction to support the weight of the vehicle and its load, it is attached to the vehicle frame by means of leaf springs. Some axles were tubular in construction.

Steering is accomplished by pivoting the wheels at the outer ends of the axle by means of STEERING KNUCKLES and KING PIN'. The construction of the steering knuckle permits it to pivot about the king pin that is firmly locked in the

axle eye. The wheels rotate on the SPINDLE.

Pivoting the wheels at the outer ends of the axle is called the ACKERMAN principle of steering and is used today on all vehicles. You may recall that in the old wagon suspension turning was accomplished by swiveling the entire front axle at the center. This suspension was simple in design and construction and operated well carrying heavy loads about the farm but did not lend itself to easy steering, higher speed operations, ride control, cornering, and the pneumatic tire.

The conventional axle design STEERING LINKAGE system—SPINDLE ARM, TIE ROD, DRAG LINK, PITMAN ARM, and STEERING GEAR—connects the two front wheels together, keeps them in proper alinement, and permits the driver to steer the vehicle from the driver's compartment. But the straight axle design did not satisfy the demands for a softer ride and an easier steering automobile. The reason is obvious. When a conventionally suspended front wheel strikes a bump in the road, the vehicle lurches upward, tilts to one side, and transmits the effects of the bump directly to the driver. Conversely, striking a hole in the pavement causes the same stiff, jarring shock.

Although a rugged and generally trouble-free suspension, the conventional axle for passenger cars was

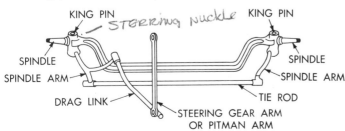

KING PIN — STEERING NUCKLE — KING PIN

SPINDLE
SPINDLE ARM
DRAG LINK
STEERING GEAR ARM OR PITMAN ARM
SPINDLE
SPINDLE ARM
TIE ROD

Fig. 1-1. A simplified drawing of a conventional front axle suspension and steering linkage. (Bear Manufacturing Company)

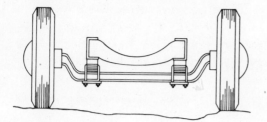

Fig. 1-2. Compared to other type suspensions, the conventional axle design did not lend itself to smooth ride with good ride control. (Bear Manufacturing Company)

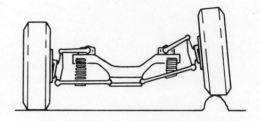

Fig. 1-4. Control arm action when coil spring compresses.

short lived. Engineers improved the "straight axle" ride by providing more flexible leaf springs and adding shock absorbers. One model utilized a *transverse* type of leaf spring arrangement that extended the width of the vehicle and stayed with the conventional axle on passenger cars until 1949. Now even many light trucks are equipped with coil springs, independent suspensions, and torsion bars.

INDEPENDENT FRONT SUSPENSION

The independent front suspension design was inevitable. The term "independent suspension" refers to the systems of springing a vehicle so that each wheel is free to move up and

down without directly affecting any other.

No axle as such is used in the independent system; the wheels are attached to the frame of the vehicle by individual linkages called CONTROL ARMS and "springing" is accomplished by COIL SPRINGS. There are two control arms on each side of the vehicle, one upper and one lower. They are connected at the outer ends by a third link, the STEERING KNUCKLE SUPPORT. It supports the steering knuckle, king pin, and spindle. Both control arms are attached at both ends by means of pivoting devices which permit free movement of the linkage in the up-and-down direction.

Note that the upper control arm is shorter than the lower control arm. This provides a difference in arc of travel of each arm and, therefore, speed of travel of movement from the pivoting point.

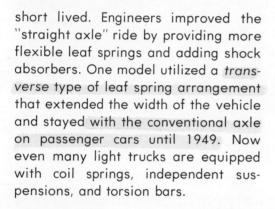

Fig. 1-3. The term "Independent Suspension" refers to the systems of springing a vehicle so that each wheel is free to move up and down without directly affecting any other. (Bear Manufacturing Company)

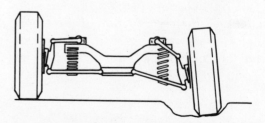

Fig. 1-5. Control arm action on rebound of coil spring.

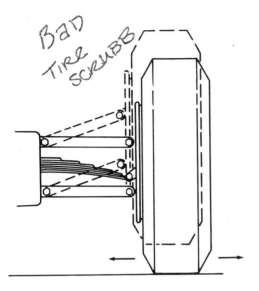

Bad Tire Scrubb

Fig. 1-6. Control arms of equal length cause tread width of vehicle to change upon spring deflection.

When the road wheel comes up due to a change in road level, the arms swing up at the outer ends and the COIL SPRING is compressed. Because the upper control arm is shorter than the lower, it moves quite rapidly in its shorter arc and allows the top of the wheel to fall inward, while the bottom of the wheel remains stationary and in contact with the road surface. The same linkage action takes place when the road wheel drops into a depression and the coil spring rebounds.

If both control arms were equal in length, the front wheels would always remain parallel to the vertical plane of the car. At every deflection of the spring, the *tread width* (distance between the two front wheels) would constantly change as the wheels passed over the road. This would cause the tires to scrub sidewise on the pavement at every bump and cause severe tire wear. (REMEMBER: whenever a tire is allowed side movement against the pavement, it causes tire wear.) The bottom of the wheel must always remain stationary to the road surface and the tread width of the vehicle must remain constant.

During "cornering," this design assists the vehicle to "bank" into a turn. On a right-hand turn, for example, the weight of the vehicle is thrown toward the outside (left); the coil spring is compressed; the upper arm rises in its arc of travel; the wheel comes in at the top and banks the vehicle against the turn. Meanwhile at the inside (right) wheel: the coil spring extends under lessened vehicle weight; the upper control arm lowers and allows the top of the wheel to come inward at the top. For one recent change in front suspension design, improved directional stability is claimed with instant steer-

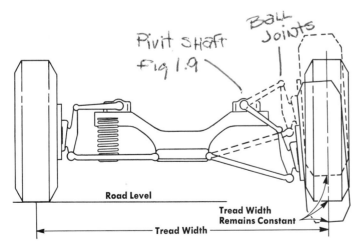

Pivit Shaft Fig 1.9

Ball Joints

Road Level

Tread Width Remains Constant

Tread Width

Fig. 1-7. Control arms of unequal length allow bottom of wheel to remain stationary to the road surface.

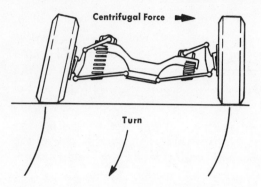

Fig. 1-8. During cornering, movement of control arms allows vehicle to "bank" into a turn.

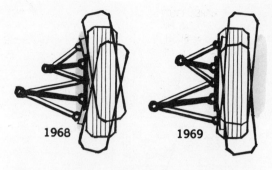

Fig. 1-10. Movement of the front wheels, at the top, differs in direction from earlier independent suspension systems. (Buick Motor Division of General Motors Corporation)

ing response, more stability in cross-winds and changes in top of wheel movement that would tend to drive another car off course. Engineers of this vehicle shifted the "instant center"—the imaginary point about which the wheel swings during deflections—moving it outside of the track. (See Figure 1-9.)

The line from the "instant center" through the center of the tire footprint continues to the vehicle's vertical center line. The crossing point is the roll center. On other cars front roll-center height varies from about 1½" below to 4½" above ground level. This design

allows roll-center height to be 3" *below* ground level.

This automobile still employs the long lower control arm and short upper control arm suspension system used in other vehicles. The difference is that the front wheels of these cars move *outward* at the top in jounce (or spring compression) and *inward* at the top in rebound. Thus, whenever the car is tilted to the right because the road slopes in that direction, the left front wheel (in jounce) leans to the left at the top, keeping the car on a straight course. The movement of the front wheels, at the top, differs in di-

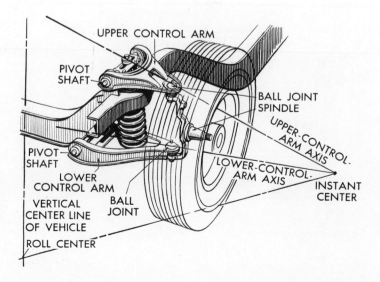

Fig. 1-9. New suspension design provides "instant center" outside vehicle track. (Buick Motor Division of General Motors Corporation)

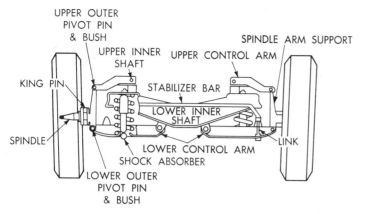

Fig. 1-11. Independent front suspension, lower coil spring mounting. (Bear Manufacturing Company)

rection from earlier independent suspension systems.

The independent front suspension system with the long and short arm design is in widespread use today. It allows independent freedom of wheel action for *best ride control* and *best tire mileage* without changing tread width. Even rear suspensions (Corvette) are being designed as independent instead of the conventional rear end housing, to gain a smoother ride.

The differences in construction of independent front suspensions are known by the manner in which the springs are mounted and the name and number of parts used.

Lower Coil Spring Mounting

The most popular method of springing the vehicle has been to mount the coil springs on the lower control arms.

Earlier independent suspension outer pivot points consisted of steel PINS and BUSHINGS. Other component parts are: UPPER and LOWER CONTROL ARM INNER SHAFTS, UPPER OUTER PIVOT PIN and BUSHING, LOWER OUTER PIVOT PIN and BUSHING, and STABILIZER BAR and LINK.

The STABILIZER BAR, mounted to the frame in rubber bushings, extends across the width of the vehicle and is attached at each end of the lower control arms by means of STABILIZER BAR LINKS. The bar adds stability to the ride of the vehicle by restricting the movement of each suspension unit. As the road wheel rises over a road obstruction, the stabilizer bar actually "twists" throughout its length, resisting the upward movement of the suspension—so the term, "stabilizer" bar. The SHOCK ABSORBER is generally mounted through the coil spring, one end firmly

Fig. 1-12. Independent front suspension, ball joint type. (Bear Manufacturing Company)

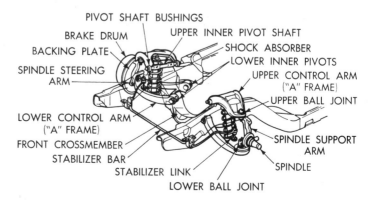

attached to the frame, the other to the lower control arm.

The purpose of the shock absorber is to dampen and control spring action and keep the wheels down on the road at all times. As its name implies, it "absorbs" shocks from the road and wheels before they reach the passenger compartment.

Ball Joint Type

Beginning in 1952 with the Lincoln car and later (1954) in all Ford cars, the outer control arm pivot points were changed from the steel pin and bushing to the BALL JOINT. The king pin and steering knuckle was eliminated, thereby reducing the number of moving parts in the independent suspension system. Today, the front wheel assemblies pivot and turn on ball joints rather than king pins. The name has been changed from the steering knuckle support to the SPINDLE SUPPORT ARM. In place of the lower control arm inner shaft, two individual INNER PIVOT BUSHINGS are used, as illustrated.

Fig. 1-13. Independent front suspension, upper coil spring mounting. (Bear Manufacturing Company)

Upper Coil Spring Mounting

There are also on our highways today suspensions in which the coil springs are mounted on top of the UPPER CONTROL ARM. Outer pivot points are ball joints as in other late model cars.

Here we see the single lower control arm with its single inner pivot bushing. Also, there is a STRUT ROD mounted at one end to the frame, and at the opposite end to the outer end of the lower control arm. The strut rod maintains lateral alinement of the lower control arm. Note that, as the wheel moves up and down, the strut rod at the frame end becomes a pivoting point, and therefore it is mounted in rubber INSULATOR WASHERS.

Torsion Bar Type

Another kind of independent suspension is the TORSION BAR type. In place of coil springs, a special heat-treated spring-steel rod or bar is used, anchored at one end to the frame side rail and at the other into a hex socket on the lower control arm.

As the road wheel and the lower control arm moves up and down over road irregularities, springing is achieved by transmitting the tension along the

NEXT COMES THE McPHERSON STRUT.

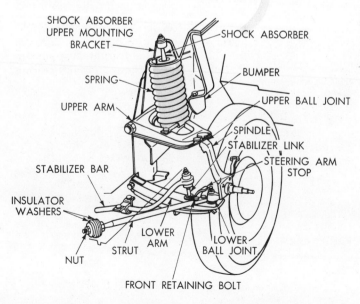

SHOCK ABSORBER UPPER MOUNTING BRACKET — SHOCK ABSORBER

SPRING — BUMPER

UPPER ARM — UPPER BALL JOINT

SPINDLE
STABILIZER LINK
STEERING ARM STOP

STABILIZER BAR

INSULATOR WASHERS

NUT — STRUT — LOWER ARM — LOWER BALL JOINT

FRONT RETAINING BOLT

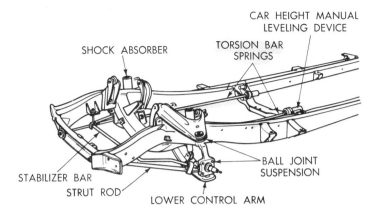

Fig. 1-14. Independent front suspension, torsion bar type. (Bear Manufacturing Company)

entire length of the bar. The bar actually *twists*, and through this twisting controls the up-and-down movement of the wheel. The operating characteristics of a coil spring and a torsion bar are alike. The difference is in shape; one is made into a coil and the other into a straight bar. Because springing is determined by the diameter and length of the rod and not by the number of coils, basic construction principles remain the same. One of the features of the torsion bar "spring" is that it can be adjusted to control car height. Torsion bar height gauges are available to aid in this adjustment.

Again, in the torsion bar suspension the single lower control arm, the single inner bushing, the strut rod, the shock absorber, and ball joints are found. The difference in construction between this suspension and others (except for the Rambler car) is that instead of the upper control arm inner shafts there are two separate pivot bushings, one at each inner end of the arm.

Cars that are equipped with this type of suspension include Chrysler products since 1957 (Chrysler, Dodge, Plymouth, Valiant, Dart, Imperial). Also, the Oldsmobile front-wheel drive Toronado and Cadillac Eldorado models have torsion bar type front suspensions. Some G.M.C. trucks were equipped with torsion bars.

Ford Twin I Beam

The Ford F-100, F-250, and F-350 series trucks represent another kind of front

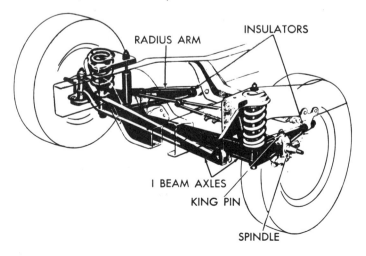

Fig. 1-15. Independent front suspension, Ford twin I-beam type. (Bear Manufacturing Company)

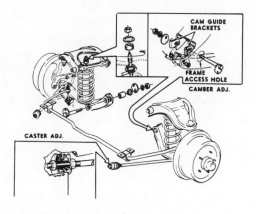

Fig. 1-16. Independent front suspension, wheel alinement adjustment means. (Bear Manufacturing Company)

independent suspension in which two I beam type front axles are used, one for each front wheel. One end of each axle is attached to the spindle and a RADIUS ARM. The other end is attached to a frame bracket on the opposite side of the truck. Coil springs are mounted between the frame spring pocket (top) and the axle.

As the front wheels encounter road obstructions, the I beam axles pivot at their inner ends, allowing each front wheel to move up and down independently of the other. The absence of upper control arms, unlike passenger car construction, requires the axles to control change in wheel position. Lateral alinement of the axles is maintained by the radius arms. Pivoting

is accomplished by rubber insulators mounted at the frame end.

Alinement Adjustment Means

To summarize the kinds of passenger car independent suspensions and their construction, all have the short upper control arm and the long lower control arm. Regardless of differences in coil spring mounting (on lower control arm or on top of upper control arm) or the use of torsion bars, the single lower control arm with its single inner pivot bushing or the inner shaft arrangement, ball joints or outer pivot pins and bushings, the object of the independent suspension is to allow each wheel to move up and down individually without affecting the opposite wheel. As we progress further in the study of front suspensions, wheel alinement angles, and adjustment procedures, you will note that means of adjustment are provided on the independent suspension to enable wheel alinement specialists to change the relative position of the wheels. The kinds of adjustments involve the use of shims, eccentrics, or strut rods and their locations in many instances differ from car to car. For example, on one model, the strut rod is adjusted for caster angle changes, while for camber an eccentric is provided at the inner pivot point on the lower control arm. The fact that means of

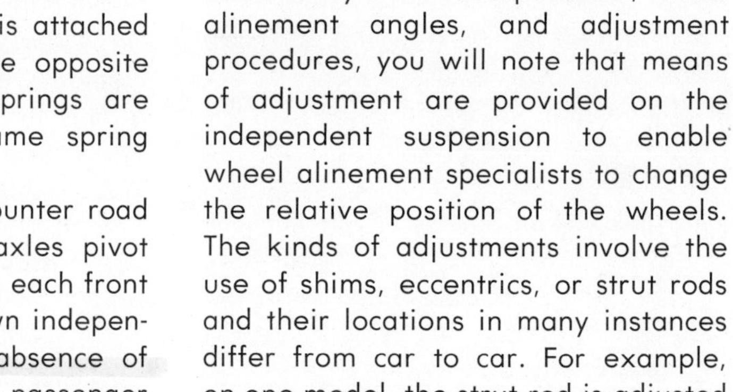

Fig. 1-17. Independent front suspension, steering linkage design—idler arm type. (Bear Manufacturing Company)

adjustment do exist on the independent suspension is all that you need to remember at this time.

Steering Linkage

With the advent of the independent suspension system, the steering linkage had to change. It was no longer possible to use the single long tie rod to connect the two front wheels as on the conventional axle design. Because the front wheels are independently sprung, the steering linkage must also be independent, one tie rod for each wheel, or one tie rod for each steering arm, pivoting near the center of the vehicle and lying in approximately the same plane as the lower control arm. Its pivot points are called TIE ROD ENDS.

The most popular steering linkage design today is the IDLER ARM SYSTEM. An idler arm is mounted to the right frame side rail opposite the PITMAN ARM. It serves to support the IDLER RELAY ROD or INTERMEDIATE STEERING ARM that connects the two as well as to support the tie rod assemblies. The TIE ROD ADJUSTING SLEEVE provides the means for adjusting toe-in and centering steering systems (steering wheels) in straight ahead position.

REAR SUSPENSION SYSTEMS

There are two basic kinds of rear-wheel suspensions in current vehicles; the Conventional Rear Housing and the Independent Rear-wheel Suspension system. Both offer various methods of springing rear wheels.

Conventional Rear Housing Suspension

The Conventional Rear Housing Suspension encloses the vehicle differential and rear-wheel axles in a rigid, tubular unit. This rear housing is attached to the vehicle frame by LEAF SPRINGS and springing is accomplished (as illustrated in Figure 1-18) by leaf springs. As the rear wheels move up and down over normal road irregularities, the suspension pivots at the front spring mounts. REAR SPRING SHACKLES permit the leaf springs to flex and change length without upsetting housing-to-frame alinement.

Some conventional rear housing suspensions, however, employ coil springs as a method of springing. Rear coil springs may be mounted on lower control arms that extend from the vehicle side rails to each outer end of the housing. See Figure 1-19.

Rear coil springs are also mounted directly on the housing itself as shown in Figure 1-20. In either instance, the rigid rear housing maintains in-and-out (toe-in) and up-and-down (camber) alinement of the rear wheels. Rear housing lateral alinement to the ve-

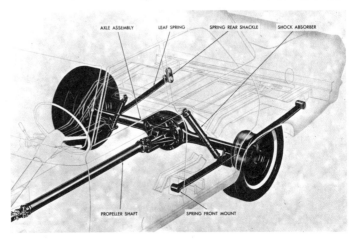

Fig. 1-18. Conventional rear housing suspension with leaf springs.

AXLE ASSEMBLY   LEAF SPRING   SPRING REAR SHACKLE   SHOCK ABSORBER

PROPELLER SHAFT   SPRING FRONT MOUNT

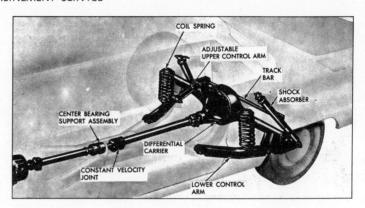

Fig. 1-19. Conventional rear housing suspension with coil springs on control arms.

hicle frame is controlled by LOWER CONTROL ARMS, LOWER CONTROL LINKS, UPPER CONTROL LINKS, TRACK BARS, or SWAY BARS.

Rear Suspension of Front-wheel-drive Vehicle

On those cars equipped with front-wheel-drive assemblies, the rear-wheel suspension consists of a straight axle and conventional, single leaf springs. Note that there are four shock absorbers mounted on this suspension to more effectively dampen rear spring action and control rear axle movement. One pair is mounted almost horizontally to the rear axle (fore-and-aft direction) and another pair is mounted vertically, as in other rear suspension systems.

Independent Rear-wheel Suspension

Some American-made vehicles provide an independent rear-wheel suspension system that allows rear wheels to move up and down independently of each other. Many employ coil springs as a method of springing or a leaf spring, as illustrated in Figure 1-22.

The leaf spring is mounted across the tread width of the vehicle and is called a TRANSVERSE LEAF SPRING arrangement. Power is transmitted to the rear wheels from the engine, propeller

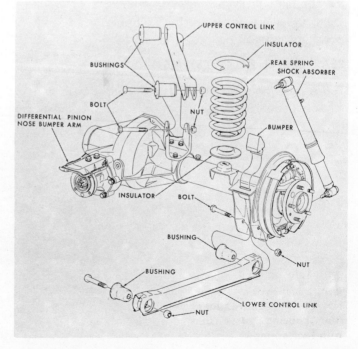

Fig. 1-20. Conventional rear housing suspension with coil springs on housing. (Cadillac Motor Car Division of General Motors Corporation)

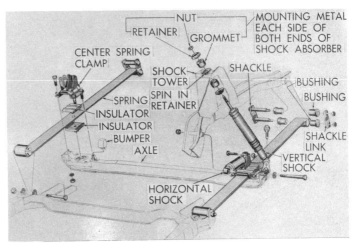

Fig. 1-21. Rear suspension design of front-wheel drive vehicle. (Cadillac Motor Car Division of General Motors Corporation)

shaft, and differential by way of REAR AXLE DRIVESHAFTS. At the ends of each driveshaft are attached universal joints hinged to provide freedom of wheel up-and-down movement. Again, to maintain lateral alinement of the rear suspension to the frame, control arms and STRUT RODS are utilized.

Some independent rear-wheel suspensions provide adjustment means (CAMBER CAMS) so that rear-wheel alinement can be adjusted much the same as front wheels. Generally, rear tire wear complaints are more common with this type of suspension than with the conventional rear housing type.

Suspension Part Groupings

The two most important factors that we must learn in our study of suspension designs and constructions are:

1. We must be thoroughly acquainted with every suspension part by name, not only so we can communicate with each other intelligently but also so we can order the correct replacement parts.
2. We must be thoroughly acquainted with each part and its relationship to others as it affects *steering*, *tire wear*, and *riding* characteristics of the vehicle. This will help us in diagnosing service problems and customer complaints.

For example, all parts representing the heavy supporting member of a front independent suspension are the UPPER and LOWER CONTROL ARMS. UPPER and

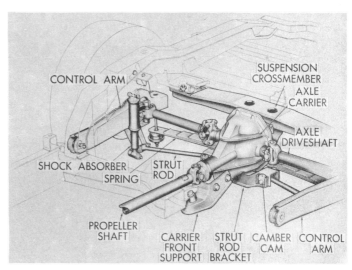

Fig. 1-22. Rear independent suspension design. (Chevrolet Motor Division of General Motors Corporation)

LOWER CONTROL ARM INNER SHAFTS or PIVOT BUSHINGS, its connecting link, the SPINDLE SUPPORT ARM, and STRUT RODS. These are "foundation" parts and if any one or more is found to be worn or defective, it may seriously impair the steering and handling stability of the vehicle.

All parts that affect the *riding characteristics* of the vehicle are the COIL SPRINGS or TORSION BARS, SHOCK ABSORBERS, STABILIZER BAR, and STABILIZER BAR LINKS.

All parts that make up the *steering components* of the vehicle are the STEERING WHEEL, STEERING GEAR, PITMAN ARM, STEERING RELAY ROD, IDLER ARM BRACKET, IDLER ARM, TIE RODS, TIE ROD ENDS, STEERING ARMS, and BALL JOINTS. Study these part groupings!

REVIEW QUIZ

For review of automotive suspension operating characteristics and part nomenclature, the following quiz is presented to test your new-found knowledge. This is a multiple-choice quiz and only one answer best completes the statement. Be selective in your choice and check against the answer sheet provided at the end of the text.

1. Independent suspensions are known by their construction and the manner in which they are sprung. Which one of the following is out of place?
   a. Torsion bars.
   b. Coil springs mounted on upper control arms.
   c. I beam axle.
   d. Coil springs mounted on lower control arms.
2. On a turn, the independent suspension system provides that:
   a. Both front wheels come "in" at the top.
   b. Only one wheel comes "in" at the top.
   c. The inside wheel moves "out" at the top.
   d. Both front wheels move "out" at the top.
3. Passenger car independent front suspension systems:
   a. All have upper and lower control arms of equal length.
   b. Have two control arms on each side of the vehicle, the lower arm always being longer than the upper arm in the short-long arm system.
   c. Have only an upper control arm if torsion bars are used.
   d. Always have the coil spring mounted directly between the upper and lower control arms.
4. Tread width is the distance between the:
   a. Outer ends of the spindles on the steering knuckles.
   b. Centerpoint of the front and rear wheels.
   c. Vertical center lines of the front tires when the wheels are on a level surface.
   d. Outer ends of the lower control arms in their normal level position.
5. In independent front suspension systems which have a steering knuckle support:
   a. The control arms are the same length.
   b. A king pin is used to attach the steering knuckle and spindle assembly to the steering knuckle support.
   c. The spindle on which the wheel rotates is forged as an integral part of the steering knuckle support.

d. Shock absorbers cannot be mounted inside the coil springs.

6. Where torsion bars are used in front suspensions:
   a. They must absorb and prevent any forward or backward motion of the front suspension as well as provide spring action.
   b. They are fitted snugly into hex sockets on the control arms and in rear anchors.
   c. They act as the pivot shaft for the lower control arm.
   d. Rotary type shock absorbers are used because the torsion bar rotates back and forth.

7. In independent front suspensions:
   a. Only one tie rod is used.
   b. An intermediate steering arm or relay rod is always used.
   c. Separate tie rods are used for each steering arm.
   d. Two tie rods of equal length are always used.

8. A front end stabilizer bar twists when:
   a. Both front wheels move up and down together.
   b. The vehicle is heavily loaded.
   c. The vehicle is traveling on a smooth surface.
   d. One spring deflects.

9. Pivoting the wheels at the outer ends of the axle is called:
   a. The reverse Elliott system.
   b. The Elliott system.
   c. The Ackerman principle of steering.
   d. The Hotchkiss system.

10. The purpose of the strut rod on independent front suspensions is to:
    a. Support the coil springs.
    b. Provide a pivoting point for the lower control arms.
    c. Maintain lateral alinement of the lower control arms.
    d. Stabilize lower control arm movement.

Directions: Various parts of an independent suspension assembly illustrated in Figure 1-23 are indicated with a letter and an arrow. Encircle the correct part name that corresponds with each identifying letter.

11. G is the:
    a. Lower control arm.
    b. Upper control arm inner shaft.
    c. Upper ball joint.
    d. Upper control arm.

12. H is the:
    a. King pin.
    b. Steering knuckle support arm.
    c. Steering knuckle.
    d. Spindle.

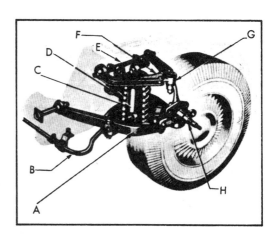

Fig. 1-23. Independent front suspension component parts.

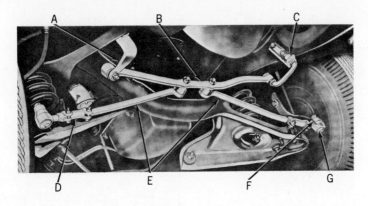

Fig. 1-24. Independent front suspension steering linkage component parts.

13. B is the:
    a. Stabilizer bar.
    b. Stabilizer bar link.
    c. Stabilizer bar mount bracket.
    d. Torsion bar.

14. E is the:
    a. Upper control arm.
    b. Upper control arm pivot pin and bushing.
    c. Upper control arm mounting bracket.
    d. Upper control arm inner shaft.

15. C is the:
    a. Shock absorber.
    b. Coil spring.
    c. Rubber bumper.
    d. Lower control arm.

Directions: Various parts of a steering linkage assembly illustrated in Figure 1-24 are indicated with a letter and an arrow. Encircle the correct part name that corresponds with each identifying letter.

16. A is the:
    a. Idler arm.
    b. Pitman arm.
    c. Idler relay rod.
    d. Steering gear.

17. F is the:
    a. Tie rod end.
    b. Tie rod end locking nut.
    c. Tie rod adjusting sleeve.
    d. Spindle steering arm.

18. E is the:
    a. Idler relay rod.
    b. Tie rod.
    c. Tie rod end.
    d. Idler arm.

19. D is the:
    a. Tie rod adjusting sleeve.
    b. Tie rod.
    c. Spindle steering arm.
    d. Idler arm bracket.

20. A steering component part that affects the steering operation of a vehicle is the:
    a. Ball joint.
    b. Spindle support arm.
    c. Strut rod.
    d. Stabilizer bar.

Chapter 2
INSPECTING THE VEHICLE·

Since professional Wheel Alinement is truly a *complete* service, it is imperative that steering and suspension component parts be thoroughly inspected and worn or loose parts replaced *before* the Wheel Alinement *adjustment* operation. Any worn or excessively loose parts must be replaced to ensure and maintain a *true alinement* job, to assure maximum *tire mileage*, and to assure *safety* in operation of the vehicle. Wheel Alinement results are directly related to the condition of front end parts.

To render professional service to customers, an Inspection Report should be completed and attached to every job order. Only after proper inspection of the steering and suspension system can you analyze the condition of the vehicle and intelligently inform the customer of the proper corrective measures required.

SPECIALIST'S CHECK LIST FOR PERFORMING WHEEL ALINEMENT SERVICES

Check off when completed:
- ____ (1) Wheel Alinement Test (Scuff Gauge)
- ____ (2) Test Rear Wheels in Same Manner
- ____ (3) Tire Condition
- ____ (4) Air Pressure
- ____ (5) Bent Wheels and Wheel Bearings
- ____ (6) Wheel Balance
- ____ (7) Shock Absorbers
- ____ (8) Drive Vehicle on Wheel Alinement Machine to Complete the Steering and Suspension Inspections
- ____ (9) Spring Sag
- ____ (10) Torsion Bar Height
- ____ (11) Steering Linkage. Jack Front End to Raise Both Wheels from Wheel Alinement Machine
- ____ (12) Inspect for Looseness of Tie Rod Ends, Idler Arm, Relay Rod Connections, Drag Link, Upper and Lower Control Arm, Inner Shaft Mounting Bolts
- ____ (13) Steering Gear
- ____ (14) Ball Joints. It may be necessary to lower one wheel and inspect one side at a time
- ____ (15) Wheel Bearing Looseness and Ball Joint Radial Checks
- ____ (16) Lower Wheel to Turning Radius Gauge, if necessary, and Repeat Inspection on Other Side
- ____ (17) Tracking
- ____ (18) Pedal Depressor
- ____ (19) Wheel Alinement Angles

Inspection Routine

It is most important that you, as a specialist, establish a routine, step-by-step inspection procedure. This

STEERING ALINEMENT INSPECTION REPORT

Name_____ _____19_____

Address_____License No._____Speedometer_____

Phone_____Make_____Body Type_____Year and Model_____

Inspection and checks made with Bear Precision Gauges and all corrections are made with Bear Equipment.

	LEFT FRONT		RIGHT FRONT		LEFT REAR		RIGHT REAR	
	OK	Not OK	OK	Not OK	OK	Not OK	OK	Not OK
Tire Condition								
Air Pressure in Tires								
Wheel Balance (All)								
Wheel Bent or Eccentric								
Wheel Bearings								
Shock Absorbers								

STEERING GEAR	Adjust	Overhaul	LEFT		RIGHT			LEFT		RIGHT	
			OK	Not OK	OK	Not OK		OK	Not OK	OK	Not OK
Torsion Bar Height							Upper Inner Shaft and Bushings				
Spring Sag or broken							Lower Inner Shaft and Bushings				
Drag Link							Spindle Supports				
Tie Rod Ends							King Pins				
Idler Arm							Upper Outer Pins and Bushings				
Ball Joint Upper							Lower Outer Pins and Bushings				
Ball Joint Lower							Spindle Limit (.005)				

FRONT ALINEMENT CHECK				FACTORY STANDARD	REAR HOUSING CHECK		
Toe-in	IN		OUT	in.	Toe-in	IN	OUT
Camber	Left	°	Right	°	°	Camber	Left °	Right °
Caster	Left	°	Right	°	°	Drive Shaft		
Turning Radius	Left	°	Right	°	°			
King Pin Indication	Left	°	Right	°	°			

FRAME CHECK		
Sideway		Mash
Sag		Diamond
		Twist
Tracking		
Knee Back		

REMARKS:

_____

_____

_____

All Work Strictly Cash

Work Performed by_____Checked by_____

W. O. No._____Reg. No._____Work Authorized by:_____

Form No. 104   Furnished by BEAR MANUFACTURING CO., Rock Island, Ill.   Printed in U.S.A.

Fig. 2-1. Steering Alinement Inspection Report. (Bear Manufacturing Company)

routine should be thorough, fast, and habit-forming, designed around your wheel alinement equipment and shop layout. Vehicle inspection routines differ because equipment at hand and shop facilities differ. Each wheel alinement specialist should work out his own inspection routine.

The inspection routine in this chapter is one way of organizing the steps in a wheel alinement service job. A specialist's check list is presented, listing the inspection steps. You may wish to check each step as we proceed from one to the other and, upon completion, note the efficiency and the order of the inspecting routine.

STEP 1 — WHEEL ALINEMENT TEST (SCUFF GAUGE)

Alinement of both front and rear wheels can be checked by simply driving across the wheel alinement tester. Because of the interrelationship of all wheel alinement angles, any change in the other angles directly affects toe-in. For this reason, it is possible to get a broad, overall picture of the condition of the suspension system by checking *toe-in* first. Reading obtained is the combined rating of both wheels and is recorded in feet-per-mile side slip or "scuff." The least front wheel tire wear results when pointer registers 0 to 3 feet "IN."

STEP 2 — TEST REAR WHEELS IN THE SAME MANNER

Excessive toe-in or toe-out reveals a bent rear housing. For some rear independent suspensions, it indicates a need for adjustment. Rear wheels should register zero for best results.

Fig. 2-2. Driving vehicle across wheel alinement tester to check for front wheel misalinement conditions. (Bear Manufacturing Company)

Fig. 2-3. Checking rear wheel alinement across alinement tester. (Bear Manufacturing Company)

STEP 3 — TIRE CONDITION

All tires should be checked for signs of wear, type of wear, tread depth, breaks, cuts or bruises, and a record made.

STEP 4—AIR PRESSURE

Equalize air pressure in all four tires to recommended levels. Accuracy of all wheel alinement tests to follow may depend upon this factor.

Fig. 2-4. Spin-testing wheels to check for bent wheels and rough wheel bearings. (Bear Manufacturing Company)

Fig. 2-5. Spin-testing wheels at higher rpm to check wheel balancing. (Bear Manufacturing Company)

STEP 5—BENT WHEELS AND WHEEL BEARINGS

Slowly spin-test front wheels and check for bent wheels and out-of-round tires. In making this test, tires should be at operating temperatures. Perfect trueness is the ideal. Generally, however, 1/8" tolerance is allowed for bent wheels and 1/16" for tire run-out. As tire construction becomes more sophisticated, tolerances will become more critical. Always adhere to the car manufacturer's recommended tolerances.

During this operation, wheel bearings are checked for roughness by placing the hand on the bumper. If any roughness is detected, bearings must be cleaned and inspected. Bearings that are rumbling and grinding should be replaced.

STEP 6—WHEEL BALANCE

Jack front end at center of crossmember and spin-test each front wheel separately for shimmy or vibrations caused by unbalance. Rear wheels also should be checked for balance.

STEP 7—SHOCK ABSORBERS

Lower vehicle to the floor and work front suspension up and down at center of front bumper. (If shock absorbers are weak, the car will continue to bounce.) Next jounce the car at each end of bumper to detect differences in shock action from one side to the other. Always replace shock absorbers in pairs. Check rear of car in the same manner.

Fig. 2-6. Driving vehicle onto wheel alinement machine. (Bear Manufacturing Company)

STEP **8**—DRIVE VEHICLE ON WHEEL ALINEMENT MACHINE TO COMPLETE THE STEERING AND SUSPENSION INSPECTIONS

STEP **9**—SPRING SAG

Riding height of the automobile should be equal fore and aft and from side to side within tolerances. Springs that are sagged or unequal upset the riding and steering characteristics of the vehicle. Therefore, excessive car lean caused by unequal loadings or a damaged spring should be corrected before alining the wheels.

Measure coil and leaf spring sag conditions following specific reference points furnished by the car manufacturer. For best results, tolerances must be within specifications. Difference in spring height from one side of the vehicle to the other should not exceed 1/2". Always replace springs in pairs.

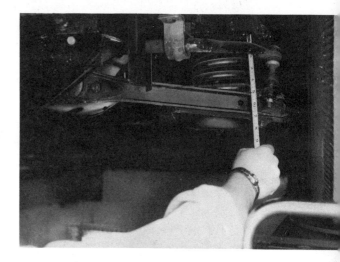

Fig. 2-7. Measuring spring height and side-to-side sag limits. (Bear Manufacturing Company)

riding height of vehicle. Torsion bar adjustments are required if height measurements do not lie within 1/8" of car manufacturer's specifications.

STEP **10**—TORSION BAR HEIGHT

For Chrysler product torsion bar–equipped suspensions, install torsion bar height gauges and measure front

STEP **11**—STEERING LINKAGE

Jack front end at outer ends of lower control arms to raise wheels from alinement machine. Be sure runway blocks

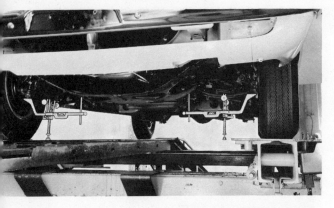

Fig. 2-8. Reading torsion bar height gauges to measure front riding height of torsion bar front suspensions. (Bear Manufacturing Company)

Fig. 2-9. Checking steering linkage from in front of the vehicle. (Bear Manufacturing Company)

are against rear wheels and brake is off. Alternately push and pull both front wheels together to inspect steering linkage for worn or loose parts. Replace worn parts. There should be no free play at the tie rod ends and relay rod connections.

STEP 12—INSPECT FOR LOOSENESS OF TIE ROD ENDS, IDLER ARM, RELAY ROD CONNECTIONS, DRAG LINK, UPPER AND LOWER CONTROL ARM, INNER SHAFT MOUNTING BOLTS (SEE ARROWS)

Another way to inspect for idler arm looseness is to grasp the idler arm and work it up and down. Looseness at the idler arm causing movement of the right front wheel in excess of 1/16" is cause for the idler arm and/or its bracket to be replaced.

STEP 13—STEERING GEAR

To check manual steering gears for roughness and "sticking," turn front wheel (preferably left front) "in" to its extreme travel position. Slowly bring wheel back through its travel noting roughness or "jumping" of the wheel.

Fig. 2-10. Observing looseness of steering and suspension parts during the checking procedure. (Bear Manufacturing Company)

Fig. 2-11. Turning front wheel throughout its travel to check manual steering gear roughness. (Bear Manufacturing Company)

turn the steering wheel slowly through its straight ahead position. A slight drag or tightness should be felt. If not, steering gear requires complete adjustment. For power steering, start the engine and check for free play when moving the steering wheel, back and forth, in straight ahead position. Check power steering pump reservoir located under hood for proper fluid level. Inspect pump drive belt adjustment. Check power steering pressure hoses for leaks, cracks, and kinks.

Action should be smooth. If it is not, remove gear and overhaul.

To inspect steering gear cross shaft bushing wear and mounting-to-frame looseness, turn wheel to extreme stop and "bounce" wheel off its stop. Movement of cross shaft indicates worn bushings. Replace bushings if back-and-forth play is excessive. Steering gear should be securely tightened to frame side rail.

Also inspect upper and lower control arm inner pivot shafts and/or bushings for looseness during this inspection operation. Replace parts if movement exceeds 1/16". Repeat on other side of car.

To check steering gear adjustment,

STEP 14—BALL JOINTS (AXIAL CHECKS—UP AND DOWN)

Inspect for looseness of ball joints, upper and lower control arm outer pins and bushings, and king pins. Lower one wheel to wheel alinement machine and inspect parts on opposite wheel. Place bar under tire and work wheel up and down. Generally, *lower ball joint stud movement should not exceed 1/16".* If there is any looseness at upper ball joint, joint should be replaced.

On cars with coil springs mounted on upper control arm, jack vehicle at lower control arm inner shaft, at the cowl, or at the crossmember. *Upper ball joint stud movement should not exceed 1/16".* If there is any looseness at lower ball joint, joint should be replaced.

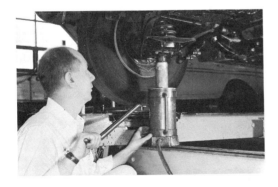

Fig. 2-12. Checking ball joint *axial* (up-and-down) free movement with pry bar. (Bear Manufacturing Company)

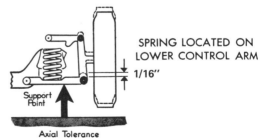

Fig. 2-13. To check ball joints (axial play) of cars with coil spring on lower arm, support wheel under control arm, as shown.

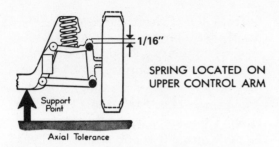

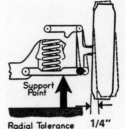

Fig. 2-14. To check ball joints (axial play) of cars with coil spring on upper arm, support front end of frame, as shown.

Always check against car manufacturer's specifications for proper tolerances.

STEP 15—WHEEL BEARING LOOSENESS AND BALL JOINT (RADIAL CHECKS—IN AND OUT)

Grasp wheel at top and bottom and work in and out. Looseness between the brake backing plate and brake drum indicates a worn or incorrectly adjusted wheel bearing. If wheel bear-

Fig. 2-15. To check front wheel bearing looseness and ball joint *radial* (in-and-out) free movement, grasp wheel at top and bottom and work in and out. (Bear Manufacturing Company)

Fig. 2-16. To check ball joint (radial play) of cars with coil spring on lower arm, support wheel under control arm, as shown.

ings are loose, adjust before checking ball joints for wear. (Do not mistake ball joint wear for wheel bearing looseness!) *If in-and-out movement exceeds 1/4" at the tire, the lower ball joint should be replaced.* There should be no looseness at the upper ball joint.

To conduct this inspection on cars with coil springs mounted on upper control arm, jack vehicle at lower control arm inner shaft, at the cowl, or at the crossmember. *If in-and-out movement at the tire exceeds 1/4", the upper ball joint should be replaced.* If there is any looseness at lower joint, joint should be replaced.

To obtain greater accuracy and better customer satisfaction, a Ball Joint Checker is used for checking ball joint wear tolerances. Replace ball joints

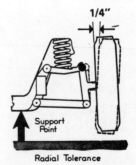

Fig. 2-17. To check ball joints (radial play) of cars with coil spring on upper arm, support front end at frame, as shown.

Fig. 2-18. To measure amount of ball joint radial movement, place ball joint checker against tire sidewall. (Bear Manufacturing Company)

if tolerances are not within car manufacturer's specifications. Always adhere to the Ball Joint Checker Manufacturer's Operating Instructions.

Careful inspection should also be made for moisture or grease on the brake backing plate. Moisture or grease indicates leaking wheel cylinders or grease retainers.

At this time also shock absorbers should be inspected for leakage, as a follow-up from the previous "bounce" test. Worn or leaking shock absorbers should be replaced in pairs.

STEP 16—LOWER WHEEL TO TURNING RADIUS GAUGE ON WHEEL ALINEMENT MACHINE — JACK OPPOSITE WHEEL AND REPEAT INSPECTION PROCEDURES ON OTHER SIDE

STEP 17 — TRACKING

With the Tracking Gauge, measure the distance between the front and rear wheels on one side of the vehicle and compare with the other side. The purpose of a tracking check is to be sure the rear wheels follow the front wheels in a parallel position. Misalinement of the frame, rear housing, or front suspension will result in unequal measurements. Allowable tolerance is 1/8". The wide use of strut rods on today's front suspensions, especially those that can be adjusted to obtain alinement settings, makes the tracking check an important measurement.

Fig. 2-19. To measure amount of ball joint axial movement, place ball joint checker against outer tie rod end. (Bear Manufacturing Company)

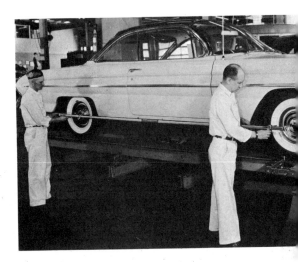

Fig. 2-20. Checking vehicle tracking with a tracking gauge compares the distance between the rear wheel and the front wheel on one side to that of the other. (Bear Manufacturing Company)

Fig. 2-21. Installing a pedal depressor to the brake pedal locks all four wheels, assuring good vehicle safety precautions and greater accuracy in wheel alinement angle readings. (Bear Manufacturing Company)

Fig. 2-22. One kind of wheel alinement gauge used to measure angles is the magnetic type of caster/camber gauge. (Bear Manufacturing Company)

STEP 18—PEDAL DEPRESSOR

As a preliminary step toward checking wheel alinement angles, place pedal depressor on brake pedal so that all four wheels are locked. This serves as an additional safety precaution to prevent the vehicle from accidentally rolling off the wheel alinement machine. The use of a pedal depressor also assures more accurate alinement readings because it keeps the front wheels from rolling on the turning radius gauges while the angles are being measured.

STEP 19—WHEEL ALINEMENT ANGLES

Check wheel alinement angle settings following the wheel alinement equipment maker's operating instructions. Record camber, caster, turning radius, and king pin inclination or steering axis inclination readings on the Inspection Report. Compare readings with the car manufacturer's recommended specifications and tolerances.

Completing the Inspection

Customer satisfaction and financial profit will depend largely on the degree of care exercised in making each of the inspection steps. A loose wheel bearing or an excessively worn ball joint will adversely affect wheel alinement settings and the maintenance of those settings for maximum tire mileage. For example, using a 14″ wheel, lateral movement of 1/16″ at the tread will affect the accuracy of the camber readings by approximately 1/4 degree. It is readily apparent that any movement in excess of 1/4″ at the tread will make it impossible for the specialist to perform a satisfactory alinement job.

Record inspection results. Report to the car owner and sell the services needed to restore the vehicle's steering and suspension system to the car manufacturer's acceptable tolerances.

STEERING ALINEMENT INSPECTION REPORT

Name_____ 19____

Address_____ License No._____ Speedometer_____

Phone_____ Make_____ Body Type_____ Year and Model_____

Inspection and checks made with Bear Precision Gauges and all corrections are made with Bear Equipment.

	LEFT FRONT		RIGHT FRONT		LEFT REAR		RIGHT REAR	
	OK	Not OK	OK	Not OK	OK	Not OK	OK	Not OK
Tire Condition								
Air Pressure in Tires								
Wheel Balance (All)		✓		✓				
Wheel Bent or Eccentric								
Wheel Bearings								
Shock Absorbers		✓		✓				

STEERING GEAR — Adjust ✓ / Overhaul	LEFT		RIGHT				LEFT		RIGHT	
	OK	Not OK	OK	Not OK			OK	Not OK	OK	Not OK
Torsion Bar Height					Upper Inner Shaft and Bushings					
Spring Sag or broken					Lower Inner Shaft and Bushings					
Drag Link					Spindle Supports					
Tie Rod Ends					King Pins					
Idler Arm				✓	Upper Outer Pins and Bushings					
Ball Joint Upper					Lower Outer Pins and Bushings					
Ball Joint Lower		✓		✓	Spindle Limit (.005)					

FRONT ALINEMENT CHECK			FACTORY STANDARD	REAR HOUSING CHECK		
Toe-in	IN	OUT	in.	Toe-in	IN	OUT
Camber	Left °	Right °	°	Camber	Left °	Right °
Caster	Left °	Right °	°	Drive Shaft		
Turning Radius		°	°			

Fig. 2-23. Completing the Inspection Report and recording all items needing attention is the final step in the checking procedure.

REVIEW QUIZ

The following quiz is designed to review vehicle front end checking procedures and many of the wear tolerances. Be selective in your choice of answers and check against the answer sheet at end of the text.

1. Before alining wheels, air pressure in tires should be:
   a. Higher in front than rear.
   b. As recommended by manufacturer.
   c. Left alone.
   d. Inflated to 35 lb.

2. Torsion bars should be:
   a. Adjusted before alining front wheels.
   b. Adjusted by car dealer only.
   c. Never adjusted.
   d. Adjusted after alining front wheels.

3. The need for front end alinement correction is generally determined by:
   a. Abnormal tire wear.
   b. Wheel balance.
   c. Road rumble.
   d. Low tire pressure.

4. A condition which can contribute to excessive movement or free play in a front wheel is:
    a. Weak shock absorbers.
    b. Worn brake drums.
    c. Sagged coil springs or weakened torsion bars.
    d. Front wheel bearings in need of adjustment.

5. A condition which can contribute to excessive lateral (side-to-side) movement or free play in a front wheel is:
    a. A worn idler arm.
    b. Loose wheel bearing adjustment.
    c. Worn pivot shafts to frame or crossmember.
    d. Loose shock absorber mounting.

6. The method illustrated here is used when checking the:
    a. Wear of tie rod ends.
    b. Lower pivot inner shaft wear.
    c. Steering gear looseness.
    d. Ball joint wear.

7. Loose and worn parts will cause:
    a. Tires to wear abnormally.
    b. Wheels and tires to bounce along the highway.
    c. Wheel bearings to fail.
    d. None of these.

8. To check ball joints on suspensions with coil springs on lower control arm, the jack is placed:
    a. Under the lower control arm inner shaft.
    b. Under the crossmember.
    c. Under the lower control arm as far outboard, toward the wheel, as possible.
    d. Under the coil spring.

9. To check ball joints on suspensions with coil springs on upper control arms, the jack is placed:
    a. Under the lower control arm inner shaft.
    b. Under the coil spring.
    c. Under the lower control arm as far outboard, toward the wheel, as possible.
    d. Under the lower ball joint.

10. In checking the ball joints, excessive movement of the front wheel (when jacked from the floor and alternately pushed and pulled at the top and bottom of the wheel) is indicated if movement is greater than:
    a. 3/8".
    b. 1/4".
    c. 1/8".
    d. 1/2".

11. When unusual wear of the rear tires is noticed:
    a. Switch tires to front wheels.
    b. Rear brake adjustment is probably unequal.
    c. Check alinement of rear wheels.
    d. Rear shock absorbers are probably weak.

PUSH IN

Alternately

PULL OUT

Fig. 2-24. Working the wheel in and out is one front suspension check.

12. To check steering gear adjustment:
    a. Turn front wheels to one side and move back and forth to detect any side play.
    b. With front wheels on floor, move steering wheel back and forth.
    c. With front wheels jacked, move wheels slowly through their straight ahead position.
    d. Jack one wheel at a time and move each wheel back and forth while in straight ahead position.

13. To conduct a ball joint *axial* check:
    a. Work the wheel in and out at top and bottom by hand.
    b. Work the wheel up and down with pry bar under the tire.
    c. Work upper control arm up and down with pry bar.
    d. Pry against the ball joint and its mounting.

14. In conducting a ball joint *radial* check, movement at the tire should not exceed:
    a. 1/2".
    b. 1/16".
    c. 1/8".
    d. 1/4".

15. Steering linkage looseness should not exceed:
    a. 1/8".
    b. 1/4".
    c. 1/16".
    d. No free play.

16. To check for leaking shock absorbers:
    a. Bounce the vehicle up and down.
    b. Bounce one side of vehicle only.
    c. Look at the shock absorbers.
    d. Rock the vehicle from side to side.

17. A tracking gauge is used to measure:
    a. A bent rear end housing.
    b. The distance between the two front wheels.
    c. A bent wheel.
    d. The distance between the front and rear wheels on both sides of the vehicle.

18. Tracking tolerance is:
    a. 1/16".
    b. 1/8".
    c. 1/4".
    d. 0".

19. Steering gear adjustment allowable tolerance in straight ahead position is:
    a. 1/2" at the steering wheel.
    b. 1/4" at the steering wheel.
    c. No free play at the steering wheel.
    d. None of these.

20. If one spring is found sagged beyond tolerances:
    a. The defective spring only should be replaced.
    b. Both springs should be replaced.
    c. Replace springs with heavy-duty springs.
    d. Aline vehicle according to present riding height.

Chapter 3
STEERING GEAR SERVICES (MINOR)

The importance of steering gear condition and adjustments to wheel alinement performance cannot be overemphasized. The servicing of steering gears, both *manual* and *power*, is an integral part of wheel alinement service.

In spite of the accuracies of wheel alinement settings that can be obtained, a worn or loose steering gear will destroy good car handling characteristics by causing the vehicle to wander and weave down the highway. On the other hand, an overtight or

---

Name_____ _____19____

Address_____License No._____Speedometer_____

Phone_____Make_____Body Type_____Year and Model_____

Inspection and checks made with Bear Precision Gauges and all corrections are made with Bear Equipment.

	LEFT FRONT		RIGHT FRONT		LEFT REAR		RIGHT REAR	
	OK	Not OK	OK	Not OK	OK	Not OK	OK	Not OK
Tire Condition								
Air Pressure in Tires								
Wheel Balance (All)		✓		✓				
Wheel Bent or Eccentric								
Wheel Bearings								
Shock Absorbers		✓		✓				

STEERING GEAR	Adjust ✓	Overhaul	LEFT		RIGHT				LEFT		RIGHT	
			OK	Not OK	OK	Not OK			OK	Not OK	OK	Not OK
Torsion Bar Height							Upper Inner Shaft and Bushings					
Spring Sag or broken							Lower Inner Shaft and Bushings					
Drag Link							Spindle Supports					
Tie Rod Ends							King Pins					
Idler Arm							Upper Outer Pins and Bushings					
Ball Joint Upper							Lower Outer Pins and Bushings					
Ball Joint Lower				✓		✓	Spindle Limit (.005)					

FRONT ALINEMENT CHECK					FACTORY STANDARD	REAR HOUSING CHECK				
Toe-in		IN		OUT	in.	Toe-in		IN		OUT
Camber	Left	°	Right	°	°	Camber	Left	°	Right	°
Caster	Left	°	Right	°	°	Drive Shaft				
Turning Radius	Left	°	Right	°	°					
King Pin Indication	Left	°	Right	°	°					

STEERING GEAR	Adjust ✓	Overhaul

Fig. 3-1. Steering Alinement Inspection Report. (Bear Manufacturing Company)

binding steering gear produces the same bad effects. It causes the vehicle to steer hard and to dart and dive to either side of straight ahead as the driver constantly "oversteers" to correct. Thus an undetected loose or tight steering gear can ruin an otherwise perfect alinement job. A steering gear in good condition and properly adjusted is one that turns freely throughout its entire travel without binding but yet is completely free of play or looseness.

MANUAL STEERING GEARS

All steering gears are enclosed and supported in a housing that is securely attached to the vehicle frame.

Steering gears are classified according to the device used for coupling the cross shaft to the worm gear. The types of manual steering gears in general use are:

1. Worm and Roller.
2. Worm and Sector.
3. Cam and Lever.
4. Recirculating ball.

Both the Worm and Roller and the Worm and Sector types of manual steering gears are known as the Gemmer gear, after the maker. The Cam and Lever manual steering gear is referred to as the Ross gear, and the Recirculating Ball type as the Saginaw.

Worm and Roller (or Sector) Types

A WORM GEAR of some type, usually concave, hourglass in design, is contained in the case and attached to the lower end of a TUBE and WORM SHAFT. The steering wheel is mounted at its opposite end. Every steering gear has a CROSS SHAFT. The cross shaft is located in the housing usually at right angles to the worm gear. The cross shaft carries a SECTOR GEAR, a ROLLER (as shown in Figure 3-2), or a LEVER that meshes with the worm gear. A cross shaft machined to form a sector gear at its inner end is commonly called a SECTOR SHAFT.

Cam and Lever Type

In the construction of Cam and Lever type gears, the worm is cut in the form of a cylindrical cam. It is called a cam because the pitch of the groove is not constant as in a worm or screw but is tapered, being narrower at the bottom. A lever is affixed to the cross shaft and lies at the side of the cam with tapered studs projecting from it. (Some levers have only one stud.) The stud

Fig. 3-2. Exploded view of worm and roller type of manual steering gear showing worm bearing adjustment shims and cross shaft adjustment screw. (Chrysler-Plymouth Division of Chrysler Corporation)

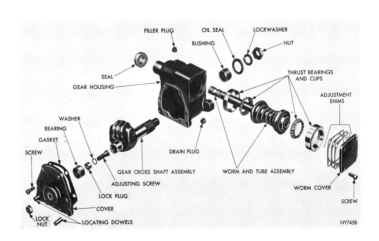

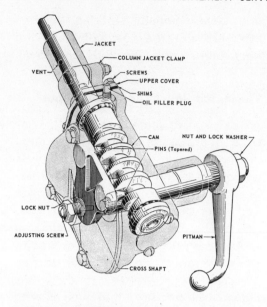

JACKET
COLUMN JACKET CLAMP
VENT
SCREWS
UPPER COVER
SHIMS
OIL FILLER PLUG
CAM
NUT AND LOCK WASHER
PINS (Tapered)
LOCK NUT
ADJUSTING SCREW
PITMAN
CROSS SHAFT

Fig. 3-3. Phantom view of cam and lever type of manual steering gear. (Bear Manufacturing Company)

fits in the cam groove so that when the cam turns, the studs move along the cam, thereby swinging the lever and turning the cross shaft.

Recirculating Ball Type

The Recirculating Ball is probably the most popular type of manual steering

gear in use today. It is the smoothest operating gear, the most trouble free, and with proper care will last the lifetime of the vehicle. The operating principles and number of adjustments are identical to those of the worm and roller type. The difference is in construction.

The gear incorporates two separate circuits of BALL BEARINGS housed in a special BALL NUT that travels up and down the worm gear. The NUT, in turn, has four tapered teeth matching corresponding teeth of the cross shaft. Instead of a roller meshing directly with the worm gear, movement is transmitted through ball bearings.

Steering Gear Operation

When the steering wheel is turned in either direction from straight ahead, the rotation of the worm gear causes instant turning of the cross shaft by way of its roller. Turning of the cross shaft turns the pitman arm and causes the complete steering linkage to move in one direction with the result that the front wheels turn in the same direction as the steering wheel.

Fig. 3-4. Cutaway view of recirculating ball and nut type of manual steering gear. (Chrysler-Plymouth Division of Chrysler Corporation)

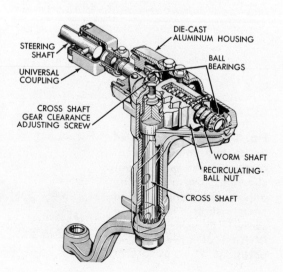

STEERING SHAFT
UNIVERSAL COUPLING
CROSS SHAFT GEAR CLEARANCE ADJUSTING SCREW
DIE-CAST ALUMINUM HOUSING
BALL BEARINGS
WORM SHAFT
RECIRCULATING-BALL NUT
CROSS SHAFT

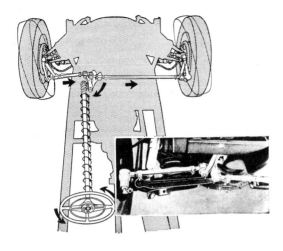

Fig. 3-5. The vehicle steering operation.

The cross shaft meshes with the worm gear in its exact center when the front wheels are in a straight ahead direction. It is at this point that the cross shaft is at its closest mesh. Because of the hourglass design of the worm gear, looseness develops in the gear as the cross shaft moves away from its center position. (The cross shaft is no longer at its closest mesh or least play.) Have you noticed this on your own car? With the front wheels turned fully in one direction, there is a great deal of steering wheel free play. This occurs because of the hourglass design of the worm gear and is not a malfunction of the steering gear.

Therefore, straight ahead direction is perhaps the most important consideration in steering services. This point of closest mesh between the cross shaft and worm gear is called *Hi-Point*.

MANUAL STEERING GEAR ADJUSTMENTS

All manual steering gears are adjustable with *adjustment procedures* differing only according to the construction and design of the gear. Regardless of make or adjustment provisions, there are three areas that must be considered when adjusting any steering gear:

1. Tube and worm shaft end play. (If the worm gear is allowed to float up and down, instant steering response will be lacking.)
2. Cross shaft end play.
3. Hi-Point or backlash between cross shaft and worm gear.

The most serious error committed by wheel alignment specialists is not making manual steering gear adjustments in their proper order of sequence. As a consequence, the entire wheel alinement service can suffer. Steering gear adjustments listed above are arranged in proper order and *must be performed strictly in sequence.*

The first adjustment is the correction of tube and worm shaft end play. The second is cross shaft end play adjustment. The third is Hi-Point adjustment. All current manual steering gears are "two-adjustment" gears, which means that (2) the cross shaft end play adjustment and (3) the Hi-Point adjustment are combined. When the Hi-Point adjustment is made, elimination of cross shaft end play is accomplished at the same time. The *first* adjustment, in proper sequence, however, remains—tube and worm shaft end play adjustment. A typical manual steering adjustment procedure is presented below.

Adjusting Worm Bearing End Play

1. Turn steering wheel to extreme travel and back one-half turn, if adjustment is performed on vehicle with gear assembled.
2. Remove or add one shim at a time

from the worm cover or end plate assembly. Steering wheel:

Holds—1/2 lb. clay weights
Drops—3/4 lb. clay weights

Note: Removing a shim increases worm bearing preload. Adding a shim decreases worm bearing preload.

To measure the amount of drag or effort to turn the steering wheel through its travel during the adjustment process, clay weights (modeling clay) are attached to the rim of the steering wheel. Car manufacturers also recommend the use of a "spring scale" or torque wrench. Always adhere to car manufacturer's specifications.

Adjusting the Hi-Point

1. Center steering gear: Turn steering wheel through its complete travel counting the number of turns. Return one-half the distance to locate midposition.

Fig. 3-6. Using a spring scale to check the amount of steering wheel drag through its travel.

2. Turn Hi-Point adjusting screw in clockwise direction until all backlash is removed.

Recirculating ball type steering gear adjustments are the same in principle. Instead of using shims for adjusting worm bearings, there is an adjusting screw. The same adjustment sequence *always* is followed: Worm bearing adjustment is first, then hi-point.

ADJUSTING STEERING GEAR IN THE CAR

Worm and Roller Type

1. Disconnect pitman arm or steering linkage.
2. Worm bearing adjustments:
   a. Turn steering wheel to either extreme travel and back one-half turn.
   b. Attach clay weights or spring scale to rim of steering wheel.
   c. Remove or add one shim at a time from end plate assembly located at lower end of gear case until steering wheel:

LIGHT VEHICLE   HEAVY VEHICLE
Holds—1/2 lb.   Holds—3/4 lb.
Drops—3/4 lb.   Drops—1 lb.

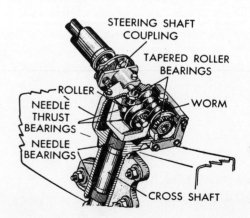

Fig. 3-7. Cutaway view of worm and roller type of manual steering gear. (Bear Manufacturing Company)

Removing a shim increases worm bearing preload; adding a shim decreases worm bearing preload. On Ford-type gears, shims are located at top end of gear case.

3. Backlash or Hi-Point adjustment:
    a. Center steering gear: Turn steering wheel through its complete travel and count the number of turns. Return one-half the distance to locate midposition.
    b. Attach vise grips to cross shaft splines or move pitman arm back and forth to determine amount of backlash.
    c. Remove lock nut and star washer from Hi-Point adjusting screw located on cross shaft cover assembly. Turn adjusting screw in clockwise direction until all backlash is removed.
    d. Reinstall star washer marked "this side out" making certain it fits snugly about the raised boss of the cover assembly. Reinstall lock nut and tighten securely.

4. Reinstall pitman arm or steering linkage with front wheels in straight ahead position. Refill steering gear with recommended gear lube to bottom of filler plug hole or as recommended by the vehicle manufacturer.

Cam and Lever Type

1. Disconnect pitman arm or steering linkage.
2. Worm bearing adjustment:
    a. Turn steering wheel to either extreme travel and back one-half turn. Attach clay weights or spring scale to rim of steering wheel.
    b. Remove or add one shim at a

time between end plate assembly and gear case until steering wheel:

LIGHT VEHICLE	HEAVY VEHICLE
Holds—1/2 lb.	Holds—3/4 lb.
Drops—3/4 lb.	Drops—1 lb.

Removing a shim increases worm bearing preload. Adding a shim decreases worm bearing preload.

Caution: Do not attempt to pry end plate assembly to gain clearance. Upper and lower snap rings on tube and worm shaft may become dislodged, requiring removal of steering gear to repair.

3. Backlash or Hi-Point adjustment:
    a. Center steering gear: Turn steering wheel through its complete travel and count the number of turns. Return one-half the distance to locate midposition.

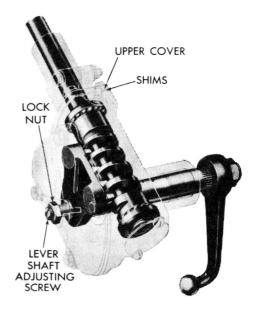

Fig. 3-8. **Phantom view of cam and lever type of manual steering gear. (Bear Manufacturing Company)**

b. Attach vise grips to sector shaft splines or move pitman arm back and forth by hand to determine amount of backlash.

c. Loosen adjusting screw lock nut on cover assembly and turn adjusting screw in clockwise direction until all backlash is removed.

d. Hold adjustment; tighten lock nut; recheck adjustment.

4. Reinstall pitman arm or steering linkage with front wheels in straight ahead position. Fill steering gear with recommended gear lube to bottom of filler plug hold or as recommended by the vehicle manufacturer.

Recirculating Ball and Nut Type

1. Disconnect pitman arm or steering linkage.

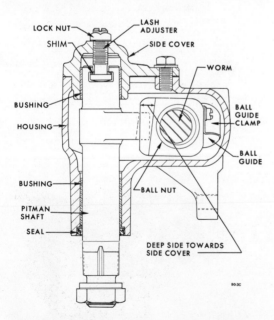

Fig. 3-9. Cutaway view of recirculating ball and nut type of manual steering gear showing "lash" adjuster location. (Buick Motor Division of General Motors Corporation)

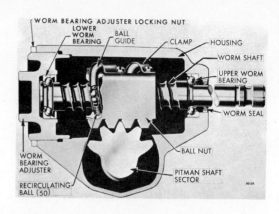

Fig. 3-10. Cutaway view of recirculating ball and nut type of manual steering gear showing worm bearing adjuster location. (Buick Motor Division of General Motors Corporation)

2. Worm bearing adjustment:
   a. Turn steering wheel to either extreme travel and back one-half turn.

   b. Using hammer and long taper punch, loosen lock nut of worm bearing adjusting screw located on end plate assembly.

   c. Attach clay weights or spring scale to rim of steering wheel. Turn worm bearing adjusting screw in clockwise direction until steering wheel:

LIGHT VEHICLE	HEAVY VEHICLE
Holds—1/2 lb.	Holds—3/4 lb.
Drops—3/4 lb.	Drops—1 lb.

3. Hold adjustment; tighten lock nut; recheck adjustment.

4. Backlash or Hi-Point adjustment:
   a. Center steering gear: Turn steering wheel through its complete travel and count the number of turns. Return one-half the distance to locate midposition. Loosen Hi-Point adjusting screw lock nut.

   b. Attach vise grips to sector shaft splines or move pitman arm back and forth by hand to determine amount of backlash.

c. Turn Hi-Point adjusting screw in clockwise direction until all backlash is removed. Hold adjustment; tighten lock nut; recheck adjustment.

5. Reinstall pitman arm or steering linkage with front wheels in straight ahead position and check steering gear lube level. Bring level to bottom of filler plug hole or as recommended by the vehicle manufacturer.

POWER STEERING GEARS

Introduction

Power steering has been used for a number of years on heavy duty applications, but it is only in recent years that power steering has been applied to any extent on passenger cars. It is estimated that today over 80 percent of passenger cars in use are equipped with power steering. With the widespread adoption of power steering, it becomes increasingly important for everyone in the automotive field to know how these units operate, what can go wrong with them, and how they are repaired.

The principle of power steering is very simple: A booster arrangement is provided which is set into operation when the steering wheel shaft is turned. The booster then takes over and does most of the work of steering. In the hydraulic power steering system, a continuously operating pump provides hydraulic pressure when needed. As the steering wheel is turned, valves are operated that admit this hydraulic pressure to a cylinder. Then the pressure causes a piston to move and the piston does most of the steering work.

Basically, there are two types of power steering systems:

1. The INTEGRAL or combined gear (valve body and power application designed into one housing—see Figure 3-11).

2. The LINKAGE type (control valve and power cylinder attached to the steering linkage system of the vehicle in addition to the conventional manual steering gear box).

Both power steering systems require a pressure pump in satisfactory operating condition to supply adequate oil pressure to the unit.

Fig. 3-11. Cutaway view of Saginaw in-line power steering gear (integral type). (Bear Manufacturing Company)

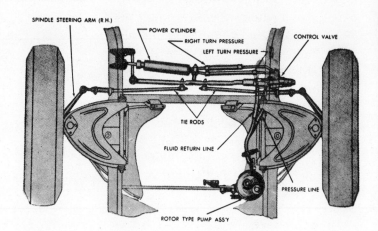

Fig. 3-12. Linkage type of power steering arrangement. (Bear Manufacturing Company)

Power Steering Service

The need for power steering service and correction is usually determined through customer complaints or a road test check, rather than in a preplanned safety inspection procedure. Some of the most common complaints affecting all hydraulically operated power gears are:

1. Fluid leaks.

2. Pump noise or pump drive belt noise.
3. Poor return of steering wheel following a turn.
4. Car pulls to one side.
5. Hard steering in either direction, especially when parking.

In many instances, these complaints can be corrected through minor adjustments and repairs of the power steer-

Fig. 3-13. Power steering pump and reservoir. (Bear Manufacturing Company)

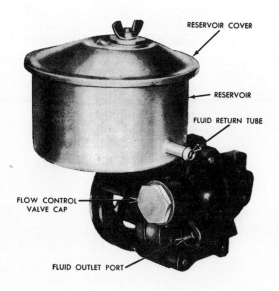

ing system and/or through front suspension and wheel alinement services. Serious and more complicated malfunctions of power steering units that require disassembly, overhaul, and major adjustment procedures are directed to the power steering specialist after normal corrective measures have been performed and trouble still persists. The following wheel alinement services will eliminate minor difficulties:

1. Check and fill pump reservoir to proper level with recommended power steering fluid.
2. Check pump drive belt condition (cracked, grease soaked, out of adjustment) and replace and/or adjust as needed.
3. Check power steering pressure hoses for leaks, cracks, and kinks. Replace leaky and defective hoses.
4. Check manual steering gears for looseness (linkage type power steering installations) and adjust gear.

Reservoir Fluid Level

If fluid is below the oil level mark on the reservoir, or low as indicated by a dipstick, add fluid to "full" mark. Do not overfill.

Belt Tension

There are two methods by which belt tension can be checked: Use a torque wrench or hook gauge to measure deflection of a belt (follow car manufacturer's specifications) or measure belt tension by thumb pressure midway between pulleys. Belt deflection should be between 1/4 and 1/2". In the absence of a gauge, the wheels may be turned full right or left to the wheel stop to determine whether the pump stops or the belt squeals. In either case, adjustment is necessary. Belt tension is correct when at extreme turn engine idle rpm drops and belt does not squeal.

Caution: Do not hold wheels against stops.

To adjust belt tension, loosen the belt pivot and adjusting bolts on pump mounting brackets to allow movement of the bracket in its adjusting slot.

Bleeding Systems

To bleed the system, raise front wheels and run engine at idling speed until normal operating temperatures are obtained. Then accelerate the engine and turn front wheels to right and left several times until bubbles in reservoir disappear. Do not hold wheels against stops. Always recheck and replenish fluid in reservoir after bleeding.

TROUBLE SHOOTING GUIDE

Fluid Leaks

CAUSE

1. Loose hose connections
2. Damaged hose
3. Too much oil in reservoir
4. Defective seals

CORRECTION

1. Tighten securely
2. Replace hose
3. Fill to proper level
4. Refer car owner to specialist

Noisy Pump*

CAUSE

1. Low oil level
2. Loose drive belt or pulley
3. Defective pump or relief valves, or worn bearings

CORRECTION

1. Fill to proper level
2. Adjust or replace
3. Refer car owner to specialist

*Slight gear noise is normal, especially on turns. A slight "hissing" noise is also normal, particularly when parking.

A "squeal" is normal on some types at extreme turns or against stops.

Caution: Do not hold at this position for an extended length of time. Extreme heat and pressure build up at this position.

Poor Steering Return

CAUSE

1. Underinflated tires
2. Incorrect alinement angles
3. Tight steering linkage
4. Sticking valves or defective steering gear

CORRECTION

1. Inflate to proper pressures
2. Aline front system
3. Replace defective parts
4. Refer car owner to specialist

Car Pulls to One Side

CAUSE

1. Incorrect alinement angles
2. Unequal tire pressures
3. Worn tires
4. Maladjusted brakes
5. Worn or binding steering and suspension parts
6. Inoperative power steering valves
7. Maladjusted directional control

CORRECTION

1. Aline front system
2. Inflate to proper pressures
3. Replace tires
4. Adjust brakes
5. Replace parts

6. Refer car owner to specialist
7. Refer car owner to specialist

Hard Steering in Either Direction

CAUSE

1. Low oil level
2. Loose drive belt
3. Underinflated tires
4. Incorrect alinement angles
5. Dry or binding steering linkage
6. Low oil pressure

CORRECTION

1. Fill to proper level
2. Adjust belt properly
3. Inflate to proper pressures
4. Aline system
5. Lubricate and free parts
6. Refer car owner to specialist

REVIEW QUIZ

The following quiz is designed to help you review the different kinds of steering gears and adjustment procedures. Be selective in your choice of answers and check against the answer sheet at the end of the text. Only one answer is correct.

Directions: Answer by encircling the letter corresponding to the correct component part.

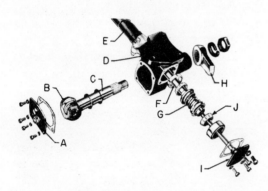

Fig. 3-14. Exploded view of worm and roller type of manual steering gear showing component parts. (Chrysler-Plymouth Division of Chrysler Corporation)

1. G is the:
    a. Rack and pinion.
    b. Recirculating ball nut.
    c. Cross shaft.
    d. Worm gear.
2. I is the:
    a. Housing cap.
    b. Worm cover.
    c. Housing.
    d. Tube and worm shaft.
3. C is the:
    a. Cross shaft assembly.
    b. Tube and worm shaft.
    c. Sector gear.
    d. Roller.

4. B is the:
    a. Sector gear.
    b. Lever gear.
    c. Roller.
    d. Cross shaft.
5. The most popular manual steering gear in use is the:
    a. Recirculating ball type.
    b. Cam and lever type.
    c. Worm and sector type.
    d. Linkage type.
6. With the front wheels in straight-ahead direction, permissible free play at the steering wheel is:
    a. 1/2".
    b. 1".
    c. No free play.
    d. None of these.
7. The steering gear adjustment that eliminates free play in straight ahead direction is known as:
    a. Cross shaft end play adjustment.
    b. Hi-Point adjustment.
    c. Worm bearing adjustment.
    d. Recirculating ball adjustment.
8. The cross shaft of a recirculating ball nut steering gear employs:
    a. A roller gear.
    b. A cam and lever gear.
    c. Roller bearings.
    d. A sector gear.
9. To properly adjust a steering gear, the first adjustment must be:
    a. Hi-Point adjustment.
    b. Cross shaft end play adjustment.
    c. Worm bearing preload adjustment.
    d. Ross gear adjustment.
10. Steering gear adjustments conducted in proper sequence give best results. Which one is *not* in proper order?
    a. Tube and worm shaft end play adjustment.

      b. Hi-Point adjustment.

      c. Cross shaft end play adjustment.

11. Most of today's manual steering gears are called two-adjustment gears. Which adjustment has been eliminated and combined with another?

      a. Cross shaft end play adjustment.

      b. Tube and worm shaft end play adjustment.

      c. Hi-Point.

12. The Gemmer steering gear is a:

      a. Cam and lever type.

      b. Recirculating ball type.

      c. Worm and roller type.

      d. Ross gear.

13. In checking a manual **steering** gear for proper adjustment, you:

      a. Raise the front wheels and move the pitman arm back and forth.

      b. Disconnect the pitman arm and turn the steering wheel to its extreme travel.

      c. raise the front wheels and move the wheels slowly through straight ahead position.

      d. Raise the front wheels and "bounce" one wheel off its stop.

14. In the linkage type power steering system the:

      a. Cross shaft is moved directly by the power cylinder.

      b. Control valve is attached to the steering gear housing.

      c. Power piston rod is attached to the vehicle frame and the power cylinder moves.

      d. Control valve assembly cannot be built into the power cylinder.

15. When making any adjustment on a manual steering gear, one precaution must always be observed:

      a. Steering linkage should be disconnected from the pitman arm.

      b. Front wheels must be raised off the shop foor.

      c. Front tires should be inflated to the correct pressures.

      d. Disconnect the horn wire to prevent accidental horn operation.

16. A manual steering gear that checks "rough" throughout its entire travel may be a cause of:

      a. A pit or gouge in the worm gear.

      b. Defective worm bearings.

      c. A defective cross shaft grease seal.

      d. Poor adjustment.

17. Removing a shim when adjusting tube and worm shaft end play causes:

      a. An increase in preload on the worm bearings.

      b. A decrease in preload on the worm bearings.

      c. Less travel of the adjuster nut in the end plate.

      d. Looseness between roller and worm gear mesh.

18. The end of the steering gear cross shaft which is outside of the housing is provided with splines for the attachment of the:

      a. Drag link.

      b. Tie rod.

      c. Relay rod.

      d. Pitman arm.

19. In the recirculating ball type steering gear:
   a. The worm nut meshes directly with the worm.
   b. All of the balls are always in the worm grooves.
   c. The sector gear is directly driven by the worm.
   d. The gear rack on the worm nut drives the sector gear.

20. The Ross gear is a:
   a. Recirculating ball type.
   b. Worm and roller type.
   c. Cam and lever type.
   d. Rack and pinion type.

Chapter 4
WHEEL BALANCING SERVICES

INTRODUCTION

No wheel alinement service may be considered complete unless the wheels are balanced. It has been said that a wheel out of balance as little as one ounce, at 60 miles per hour is comparable to strapping a 12-lb. weight to one spot on the tire. One can imagine the destructive forces that work against the tire, the wheel assembly, and the steering and suspension system. And, with our vast network of super highways and high performance vehicles, who does not drive 60 mph, at some point today?

STEERING ALINEMENT INSPECTION REPORT

Name_____ 19_____

Address_____ License No._____ Speedometer_____

Phone_____ Make_____ Body Typo_____ Year and Model_____

Inspection and checks made with Bear Precision Gauges and all corrections are made with Bear Equipment.

	LEFT FRONT		RIGHT FRONT		LEFT REAR		RIGHT REAR	
	OK	Not OK	OK	Not OK	OK	Not OK	OK	Not OK
Tire Condition								
Air Pressure in Tires								
Wheel Balance (All)		✓		✓				
Wheel Bent or Eccentric								
Wheel Bearings								
Shock Absorbers		✓		✓				

STEERING GEAR	Adjust ✓	Overhaul	LEFT		RIGHT				LEFT		RIGHT	
			OK	Not OK	OK	Not OK			OK	Not OK	OK	Not OK
Torsion Bar Height							Upper Inner Shaft and Bushings					
Spring Sag or broken							Lower Inner Shaft and Bushings					
Drag Link							Spindle Supports					
Tie Rod Ends							King Pins					
Idler Arm						✓	Upper Outer Pins and Bushings					
Ball Joint Upper							Lower Outer Pins and Bushings					
Ball Joint Lower				✓		✓	Spindle Limit (.005)					

FRONT ALINEMENT CHECK					FACTORY STANDARD	REAR HOUSING CHECK		
Toe-in		IN		OUT	in.	Toe-in	IN	OUT
Camber	Left	°	Right	°	°	Camber	Left °	Right °
Caster	Left	°	Right	°	°	Drive Shaft		
Turning Radius	Left	°	Right	°	°			
King Pin Indication	Left	°	Right	°	°			

	OK	Not OK
Wheel Balance (All)		✓

Fig. 4-1. Steering Alinement Inspection Report. (Bear Manufacturing Company)

Also, to add to the confusion and controversy surrounding wheel balancing, the driver himself may or may not detect the need for balancing his car's wheels, even at 60 mph. The "soft-riding" suspensions, or rather, suspensions engineered to reduce vibrations and keep the effects of road shock to a minimum, plus power steering, do much to absorb the effects of out-of-balance conditions of the wheel assemblies before noticeable vibrations reach the passenger compartment. But unbalanced wheels cause pounding forces, whether or not the driver feels them. It is safe to assume that almost any wheel without a wheel weight on it needs balancing. An unbalanced wheel will shorten tire life, literally pound out lubrication, and shorten the life of steering and suspension parts as well.

Conversely, wheels in proper balance will provide a smoother ride and greater vehicle stability by keeping the wheels on the pavement at any speed. Balanced wheels will correct high-speed shimmy (a sometimes violent back-and-forth shake of the steering wheel) and high-speed vehicle vibrations caused by unbalanced wheel assemblies.

Wheel balancing because of smaller wheels, wider tires, greater speeds,

Fig. 4-3. Illustrating the back-and-forth, "wiggle" action of a dynamically unbalanced wheel assembly. (Bear Manufacturing Company)

coil spring rear suspensions, and in some instances, rear independent suspensions, has become a necessity rather than a luxury. More and more the practice is to balance all four wheels of the vehicle rather than balancing the front wheels only.

How often do wheels need balancing or rechecking for balance? Tires should be checked for balance under any of the following conditions:

1. Loss of a wheel weight.
2. Flat tire.
3. Abnormal tire wear, causing a change in tires.
4. Whenever mounting new tires.
5. Whenever tires and wheels are rotated or relocated on the vehicle. (This depends upon the type of balancer used at the time of the initial balance.)
6. Normal tire wear. Wheels should be checked for balance and rebalanced once a year, or approximately every 10,000 miles.

Some wheel balancers balance entire wheel assemblies—hub, drum, wheel, and tire. In this practice, tire and wheel rotation to a different location on the car will disturb the original balance because the tire and wheel were mated to a different drum. The assembly that was balanced as a unit has been divided and is no longer the original as-

Fig. 4-2. Illustrating the up-and-down, "bounce" action of a statically unbalanced wheel assembly. (Bear Manufacturing Company)

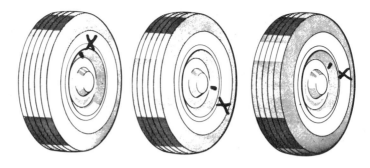

Fig. 4-4. Static balance is achieved when the wheel will not rotate by itself regardless of the position in which the wheel is placed on its axle. (Bear Manufacturing Company)

sembly. In fact, removing a wheel and tire from the wheel studs and reinstalling it, beginning with a different stud will disturb the balance of the entire assembly. That is why it is always good practice to mark (chalk) the wheel and a wheel lug when removing a wheel for any reason. Then the wheel can be reinstalled in its original position on the drum. It is not unusual for an automobile to have no shimmy or vibration before services requiring wheel removal, but following the service the car returns with a shimmy or vibration and a wheel balance problem.

WHAT IS WHEEL BALANCING?

Wheel balancing is the placement of wheel weights around a tire and wheel assembly to counteract the centrifugal forces acting upon the heavy areas. A properly balanced wheel will roll smoothly at varying speeds, without hop or wiggle caused by unbalance.

There are two kinds of balance: *static* and *dynamic*.

Static Balance — *at rest*

Static balance is balancing a wheel at rest. When a compensating weight is added to offset a heavy area of the wheel, static balance is achieved when the wheel will not rotate by itself regardless of the position in which the wheel is placed on its axis. This is true whether the wheel is mounted vertically, as on a spindle or balancer shaft, or horizontally, as on a bubble type of balancer.

A wheel that does have a static unbalanced condition because of a heavy spot will tend to rotate by itself until the heavy portion is down. To balance against the heavy portion, a weight is attached to the wheel directly opposite the heavy area. Some advocate placing the weight on the inside of the wheel. Some advocate placing the weight on

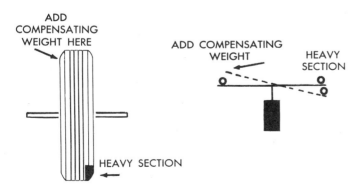

ADD COMPENSATING WEIGHT HERE

HEAVY SECTION

ADD COMPENSATING WEIGHT

HEAVY SECTION

Fig. 4-5. A wheel that is unbalanced statically will tend to rotate by itself until the heavy section is down. (Bear Manufacturing Company)

the outside of the wheel. Still others recommend placing two equal weights, one on each side of the wheel, opposite the heavy area. Also, in the case of static balancers or bubble-type balancers, one manufacturer recommends static balancing a wheel using four weights—two equal weights on each side of the wheel, at equal distances from the center of the light area.

Regardless of method followed, it is always good practice to "split" the added weight, placing an equal amount on each side of the wheel at the light area because of the other kind of balance, dynamic balance. An equal amount of static weight placed on each side of the wheel will not alter dynamic unbalance, either to worsen or to correct it, if it is present. A single weight placed on one side of the wheel, however, may induce greater dynamic unbalance.

Handwritten margin notes: split into an equal amount on each side.

equal amount of weight on tire on piston has no affect dynamic balance yet.

Dynamic Balance

Dynamic balance, simply stated, is balancing a wheel in motion.

Once a wheel starts to rotate and is in motion, the static weights, as illustrated in Figure 4-6, try to reach the true plane of rotation of the wheel because of the action of centrifugal force. In the attempt to reach the true plane of rotation (center of wheel), the static weights force the spindle to one side.

At 180° of wheel rotation, static weights, once again in the attempt to reach the true plane of rotation, "kick" the spindle in the opposite direction. The resultant side thrusts cause the wheel assembly to wobble or wriggle, in effect, down the highway. When severe enough, thrusts cause vibration and front-wheel shimmy.

It is possible then, for a wheel to be in balance statically and be out of balance dynamically. Therefore, it is desirable when static balancing wheel assemblies to split the static wheel weights equally and place them on each side of the wheel. This process will not alter dynamic balance.

To correct dynamic unbalance, equal weights are placed 180° opposite each

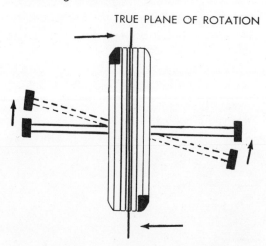

TRUE PLANE OF ROTATION

Fig. 4-6. Dynamic unbalance is caused by heavy portions of the wheel attempting to reach the true plane of rotation on every half revolution. (Bear Manufacturing Company)

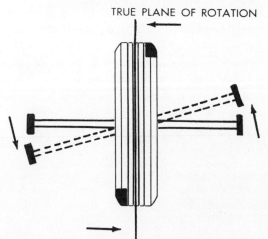

TRUE PLANE OF ROTATION

Fig. 4-7. At 180° of wheel rotation, the heavy portion of the wheel forces the spindle in the opposite direction, creating front wheel shimmy. (Bear Manufacturing Company)

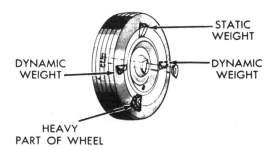

DYNAMIC WEIGHT

STATIC WEIGHT

DYNAMIC WEIGHT

HEAVY PART OF WHEEL

Fig. 4-8. To correct dynamic unbalance, equal weights are placed 180° opposite each other, one on the inside of the wheel, one on the outside. (Bear Manufacturing Company)

other, one on the inside of the wheel and one on the outside, at the point of unbalance. This corrects the "couple" action or wriggle of the wheel assembly caused by dynamic unbalance. Also note that dynamic balance is obtained while static balance remains unaffected. Likewise then, when a wheel is in dynamic balance, it is also in correct static balance.

Wheel Weights

Wheel weights are made of lead and cut to various sizes according to weight. Sizes range from 1/4 oz. to 6 oz. for passenger cars and are available up to 16 oz. for truck wheel applications. A spring-steel clip fused into the lead material at manufacture serves as the device for attaching the weight to the wheel rim. Wheel weights are installed and removed with a special hammer—plier combination tool.

Because of the increasing popularity of chrome, aluminum, and mag wheels, which do not have a conventional rim for the clip-on weight, a "tape-on" weight was developed. The tape-on weight is manufactured in flat strips of lead with an adhesive tape and tape backing attached. Much as in applying a decal, the adhesive backing is first removed. Then the weight is placed at its proper location on the wheel and firmly pressed. A light hammerblow assures correct forming to the contour of the wheel. Notice that the tape-on weight is positioned toward the center of the rim and not on the outside rim flanges, where conventional clip-on weights are fastened. One manufacturer claims that speed, snow, rain, mud, wheel cleaning brushes, and steam cleaning will not dislodge a properly installed tape-on weight.

Fig. 4-9. Wheel weights are constructed of lead and vary in size from the small (1/4 oz.) to the large (6 oz.) weights for passenger cars. (Bear Manufacturing Company)

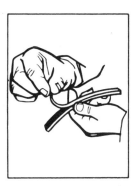

Fig. 4-10. Tape-on weights for chrome wheels are manufactured in flat strips with an adhesive backing. (Bear Manufacturing Company.)

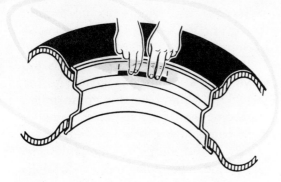

Fig. 4-11. Placing the tape-on weight near the center of the rim rather than on the rim flange. (Bear Manufacturing Company)

WHEEL BALANCERS

The three kinds of balancers in use today represent three different approaches or methods for balancing wheels:

1. Static Balancer or Bubble Balancer
2. On-the-car (Spin-type) Balancer
3. Off-the-car (Spin-type) Balancer

Each balancer or balancing method has its place in the service industry, satisfying a particular business need and doing its job well. Although balancers may differ in manufacturer and operation, all belong to one of the three categories listed above.

Static Balancer

The Static Balancer, commonly referred to as the Bubble Balancer, is designed to balance the wheel and tire assembly only, in an "at rest" or static position. The wheel and tire is removed from the vehicle and placed over the cone-shaped head. Balance is achieved by placing weight(s) on the "light" side of the wheel until the spirit level bubble located in the balancer head is centered. Generally, the weight position is marked; the wheel removed from the balancer and one-half the total balance

weight is placed on the inside of the wheel. Then the wheel is remounted and a final balance weight is placed on the outside rim flange. Following this procedure leaves the dynamic balance undisturbed.

The static balancer is used extensively in tire mounting operations when wheels have already been removed from the vehicle.

Fig. 4-12. The Micro Wheel Balancer. (The Bada Company)

Fig. 4-13. Attaching weights to a wheel that has been statically balanced. (The Bada Company)

On-the-car (Spin-type) Balancers

The on-the-car type balancer is designed to balance wheels while the wheels are spinning directly on the vehicle. Balancer controls determine amount of weight and weight location on the wheel at varying speeds of wheel rotation. The greatest advantage of this balancer is its ability to balance the entire wheel assembly including hubs and drums of front wheels and the drums of rear wheels.

On-the-car balancers are basically Static Balancers, unless a special pick-up is used, which is furnished with some models, to provide the capability of dynamic balancing too. However, within the framework of static balancing, the on-the-car balancer provides a "running-type" balance, as distinct from the bubble balancer. Controls are manipulated until all vibrations, detected by observing fenders, bumpers, and hoods, or balancer pick-up movements, have been eliminated. The wheel is then braked to a stop and the amount of weight indicated is attached to the wheel at a point determined by the balancer.

Whenever a wheel is changed to a different position on the vehicle it requires rebalancing. The change to a different hub and drum assembly is enough to leave the entire wheel assembly no longer in balance.

On-the-car balancers are used extensively for balancing rear wheels, where rear drums may be included as part of the balanced assembly. Even on those vehicles equipped with nonslip or posi-traction differentials, rear wheels may be balanced on the car. The procedure is to raise both rear wheels from the floor and remove one rear wheel from the car. At speeds of 60 mph, with transmission in "Drive" range, balance the opposite rear wheel. Reinstall wheel that was removed and balance it in the same

Fig. 4-14. An on-the-car, spin-type balancer, balancer head, and adapters to fit various wheel diameters. (Hunter Engineering Company)

Fig. 4-15. The on-the-car, spin-type balancer is designed to balance wheels while the wheel is spinning on the vehicle. (Hunter Engineering Company)

manner. (Wheel that was balanced first is left on the vehicle.)

On cars with conventional differentials, rear wheels are balanced with one rear wheel jacked from the floor, one at a time. Car speeds for balancing should not exceed 35 mph.

Fig. 4-16. On-the-car balancers are also used to balance rear wheels, where rear drums may be included as part of the balanced assembly. (Bear Manufacturing Company)

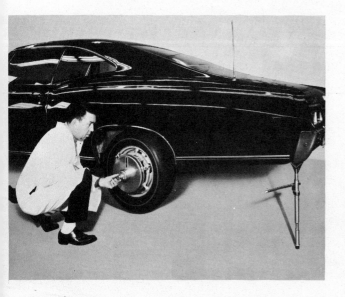

Off-the-car (Spin-type) Balancers

The third method of balancing wheels requires that front wheel assemblies (hub, drum, wheel, and tire) be removed from the vehicle and balanced off the car. This kind of balancer is a true static and dynamic balancer. The wheel assembly, with proper radius cones, is mounted on a free-floating arbor that floats on ball bearings. There are balancing indicators on each side of the arbor for interpreting amount and location of unbalance while the wheel is spinning. As with the on-the-car balancer, the rotation of wheels to different locations on the vehicle makes rebalancing necessary.

Fig. 4-17. An off-the-car, spin-type balancer is both a static and dynamic balancer that allows balancing of complete wheel assemblies (hub, drum, wheel, and tires). (Bear Manufacturing Company)

Many service centers use more than one type of balancer. The features of one are often combined with the features of another to provide flexibility in satisfying customer demands and to gain increased productivity in meeting extra work loads. Many service centers use two different balancers on the same vehicle. For example, an off-the-car spin balancer is used for front wheels and an on-the-car spin balancer is used for rear wheels. In this manner all four wheel assemblies including the brake drums are balanced, with the front wheels balanced both statically and dynamically.

Always follow the equipment manufacturer's recommended procedures for balancer operation.

REVIEW QUIZ

The following quiz is designed to help you review some of the principles of wheel balancing and its service applications. Be selective in your choice of answers and check against the answer sheet at the end of the text.

1. Wheel "hop" is generally associated with:
    a. Static unbalance.
    b. Dynamic unbalance.
    c. Out-of-round wheels.
    d. None of these.
2. To check front wheels for proper balance, you:
    a. Road test the vehicle.
    b. Jack vehicle and turn the wheels by hand.
    c. Jack vehicle and use a wheel spinner.
    d. Use a wheel balancer.
3. Wheels should be balanced:
    a. Every 5,000 miles.
    b. Every 2,000 miles.
    c. Every 10,000 miles.
    d. Every 12,000 miles.

4. Benefits of balanced wheels are many. Which item below does *not* necessarily apply:
    a. Better tire mileage.
    b. Greater steering stability.
    c. Smoother ride.
    d. Longer front end part life.
    e. Easier steering.
5. A balancer that is known to be both a static and a dynamic balancer is:
    a. A bubble balancer.
    b. An off-the-car spin type.
    c. An on-the-car spin type.
    d. None of these.
6. To static balance a wheel assembly, the compensating weight is placed:
    a. $90°$ from the heavy spot.
    b. $180°$ from the heavy spot.
    c. $45°$ from the heavy spot.
7. When static balancing a wheel, it is better to place the weight:
    a. On the inside of the wheel.
    b. On the outside of the wheel.
    c. "Split" the total weight, one-half for each side of the wheel.
    d. In none of these ways.
8. A wheel that is in balance, statically:
    a. Is also in balance, dynamically.
    b. May not be in balance, dynamically.
    c. Does not need to be in balance dynamically.
    d. Corrects shimmy.
9. To correct dynamic unbalance requires the use of:
    a. Two equal weights
    b. A single weight.

c. Two unequal weights.

d. Three weights.

10. To balance rear wheels of cars with limited-slip differentials, you:

a. Jack one side of car; balance one wheel at a time, on the car.

b. Jack both sides of car; balance both wheels at the same time, on the car.

c. Jack both sides of car; balance one wheel and remove; balance opposite wheel, then reinstall the first wheel.

d. Jack both sides of car; remove one wheel and balance the opposite wheel on the car, then, reinstall first wheel and balance.

Chapter 5
WHEEL ALINEMENT ANGLES—CASTER

There are five angles that are the foundation of wheel alinement. They are Caster, Camber, Steering Axis Inclination, Turning Radius, and Toe-in. These angles are designed into the vehicle by the manufacturer to properly distribute the weight of moving parts and to facilitate steering.

It is important that we learn what these angles are, their purposes and functions; which ones affect tire wear; which affect the steering of the vehicle; which are adjustable and which are nonadjustable. On-the-job wheel alinement adjustment procedures begin with the correction of the caster angle and end with the correction of toe-in. Car manufacturer's specifications provide a range for each angle. Good wheel alinement service maintains the five simple angles within the range of the manufacturer's specifications.

DEFINITION

The first angle is *Caster*. It is a directional control angle, which means that it is a "steering" angle and not a "tire-wearing" angle. Its definition is: *Caster is the backward or forward tilt of the king pin or ball joint at the top.*

Caster is the angle formed between true vertical (0°) and the spindle support arm as viewed from the side of the vehicle. When the spindle support arm is tilted back at the top from true vertical (toward the rear of the car), it is known as *Positive Caster.*

When the spindle support arm is tilted forward at the top from true vertical (toward the front of the car), it is known as *Negative Caster.*

PURPOSE

The purposes of Caster are:

1. To gain directional control of the vehicle by causing the front wheels to maintain straight ahead position or return to straight ahead position out of a turn.
2. To offset Road Crown.

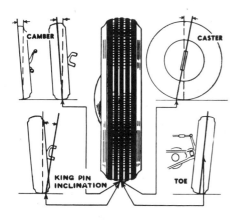

Fig. 5-1. There are five wheel alinement angles: (1) Caster. (2) Camber. (3) Steering Axis Inclination. (4) Turning Radius. (5) Toe-in. (Bear Manufacturing Company)

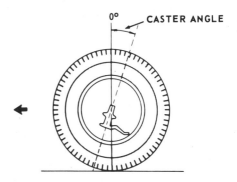

Fig. 5-2. Positive caster is the backward tilt of the king pin or ball joint from true vertical (0°) at the top. (Bear Manufacturing Company)

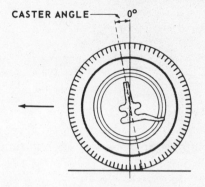

Fig. 5-3. Negative caster is the forward tilt of the king pin or ball joint from true vertical (0°) at the top. (Bear Manufacturing Company)

Caster measurements are taken from true vertical and measured in degrees. In wheel alinement, true vertical or 0° is always the starting point. All wheel alinement gauges except those for toe-in are designed to read from the 0° reference point. In thinking "degrees," imagine that we are measuring a part of a circle. A complete circle consists of 360°, starting at 0° (zero degrees, true vertical) and moving clockwise at right angles, 90°; then directly opposite (below 0°), is 180°; at the three-quarters mark, we have 270°; and finally, the completed circle is 360°.

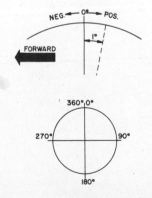

Fig. 5-4. Caster measurements are taken from true vertical and measured in degrees. (Bear Manufacturing Company)

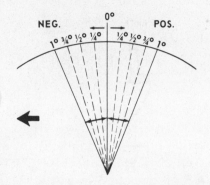

Fig. 5-5. Negative (Neg.) or Positive (Pos.) sign indicates the side of zero in reference. (Sears, Roebuck and Company)

A close-up of the top of a circle reveals an exaggerated 1° angle and its fractional parts (1/4°, 1/2°, 3/4°) on each side of zero. If you can visualize this 1° angle from a total of 360°, it presents some idea of the car manufacturer's specification "range" in which wheel alinement specialists work.

Note the fact that we are reading degrees and fractions of degrees alike on either side of zero. The only way we know on which side of zero our reference lies is by use of the negative (Neg.) or positive (Pos.) signs. You will notice, too, that on the negative side of zero, we do not read 359°, 358°, 357° — it is always 1/4°, 1/2°, 3/4°, 1°, etc., as on the positive side.

The accuracy required of wheel alinement settings should be apparent, then, because most of the time, settings are within 1/4°, 1/2°, 3/4°, or 1°. That gives an idea too, of the accuracy required in the design and construction of wheel alinement gauges and of care that is necessary in their calibration and handling.

Caster in an automobile has the same effect as the caster on furniture or shop creeper. A wheel that trails a point of load in a given direction will always follow. If we push the spindle pin of the

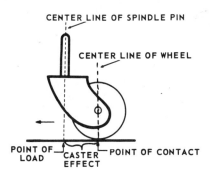

Fig. 5-6. A wheel that trails a point of load in a given direction will always follow. (Bear Manufacturing Company)

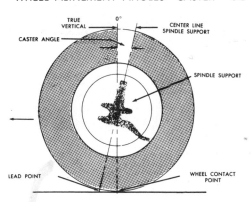

Fig. 5-8. The principle of caster is the same for ball joint or king pin suspensions. (Bear Manufacturing Company)

caster one direction, the wheel follows. If we change direction, the wheel turns about and, again, follows. The distance, then, between the point of load on the road surface (projected line through the spindle pin) to the point of wheel contact (center of wheel) represents the amount of caster effect—the smaller the distance, the less reaction of the wheel to turn about and follow in a given direction.

Caster, and more specifically *positive caster*, is the reason children are able to ride a bike with no hands on the handlebars. Because of positive caster, the wheel trails the point of load and always follows, providing forward directional control automatically.

The same principle applies to passenger cars. Positive caster (the top of the spindle support arm is back from straight up and down) places the point of load ahead of the wheel contact. This provides directional control as the vehicle travels down the highway just as the bicycle does. When we come to a corner, we have to *steer into it* because the car wants to continue in a straight ahead direction. Out of a corner, the wheels return to straight ahead direction automatically. Have you noticed that after a corner, the steering wheel winds back by itself? This is the effect of caster.

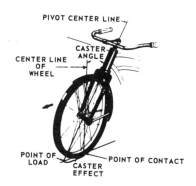

Fig. 5-7. Positive caster is the reason children are able to ride a bike with no hands on the handlebars. (Bear Manufacturing Company)

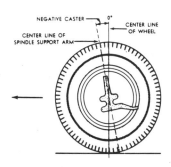

Fig. 5-9. Most passenger cars today have negative caster settings because of the influence of steering axis inclination and wider tires. (Bear Manufacturing Company)

However, most passenger cars today have negative caster specifications as established by the car manufacturer. The reason for this reverse emphasis is to obtain an easier steering automobile at slow speeds, during parking and in city driving. Remember, the point of load is behind the front wheel and we are steering "over-center" of the wheel. What of high-speed driving on a four-lane highway? Will we have good steering stability and directional control with negative caster, by itself? No. The point of load is not out ahead of the front wheels. That is why cars equipped with power steering generally have positive caster settings. (Positive caster for steering stability at high speeds, power steering for ease of steering in city driving.)

DIRECTIONAL CONTROL

The car manufacturer can achieve good directional stability and control, even with negative caster, because of the influence of another angle (Steering Axis Inclination) and the use of wider tires. Wide tires alone provide directional stability. A good example of how width affects directional control is obtained by comparing the ease with which you can roll a log in a straight ahead direction with the difficulty of maintaining straight ahead direction when rolling a hoop. The slightest tilt causes the hoop to roll to one side,

whereas the log with its wide area of contact with the road surface is more difficult to turn, tending to continue in a straight ahead direction. Consequently, the wider the tire tread, the greater the tendency for the wheel to travel in a straight ahead direction.

Out of a Turn

Caster provides good directional control in a straight ahead direction and out of a turn because of the manner in which the *spindle travels* and the reaction that takes place to the automobile once the front wheels are turned from straight ahead. Let's assume a left-hand turn with the left front wheel (driver's side) turned outward at the front. This is what takes place: with positive caster, the end of the spindle tries to lower in its swing or travel from straight ahead. Because the wheel establishes a definite distance from the end of the spindle to the ground, the end of the spindle is unable to lower and instead raises the weight of the vehicle. This takes place regardless of the direction of turn and every time the front wheels are turned from straight ahead. Consequently, the weight of the vehicle tends to force the spindles and the front wheels always to return to straight ahead position.

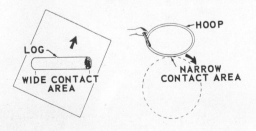

Fig. 5-10. Wide contact area to road surface increases tendency to go straight ahead. (Bear Manufacturing Company)

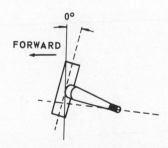

Fig. 5-11. As inner spindle moves down and back when cornering, it raises the axle or suspension and, consequently, the frame of the vehicle. (Bear Manufacturing Company)

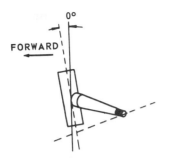

Fig. 5-12. The effects of spindle travel are opposite those for positive caster—frame will be raised when spindle is turned inward at the front. (Bear Manufacturing Company)

This happens regardless of whether the caster on a vehicle is positive or negative. Let's assume the vehicle has negative caster and we turn the left front wheel outward as before, as on a left turn. The end of the spindle *on the right wheel* (outside wheel on a turn) tries to lower; it can't; and so the weight of the vehicle is raised.

Road Crown

Every highway is constructed with some crown or pitch to allow water to run off. That is, highways are generally higher at the center than at the edges. This slant or pitch, which is commonly called *road crown*, varies in amount across the country. As the vehicle travels down the highway, its weight is thrown to the outside toward the low side of the road. If road crown is severe enough, the driver is constantly steering the vehicle toward the high side to compensate. Otherwise, the car will drift or "pull" toward the low side and off the pavement. The caster angle is used to advantage to correct against the vehicle "pulling" to one side and to relieve the driver from constantly tugging at the steering wheel to over-correct. (Remember, this is a direc-

tional control angle and not a tire-wearing angle.)

To correct against road crown pull, we place *more caster, toward positive*, on the right wheel than on the left. For example, if there is 1/2° positive caster on the left wheel, we set the right wheel to read 1° positive. The right wheel will have greater "caster effect" than the left wheel, causing the vehicle to seek the center of the road or the high side of the crown. (Positive caster creates a tendency for the front wheels to toe-in. Variations between wheels create a stronger toe-in influence of one wheel over the other.)

Rule: **The car will always pull toward the side of the leading king pin or ball joint.**

Let us suppose that both front wheels have negative caster settings. The same rule applies. We place more caster, toward positive, on the right wheel. For example, if there is 1° negative caster on the left front wheel, we set the right to read 1/2° negative. (Negative caster creates a tendency for the front wheels to toe-out. Variations between wheels create a stronger toe-out influence of one wheel over the other.) For most applications, a

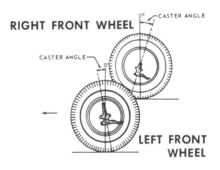

Fig. 5-13. To correct against road crown "pull," more caster toward positive is placed on the right wheel. (Sears, Roebuck and Company)

1/2° caster spread between the front wheels is sufficient to provide straight ahead direction without requiring undue effort on the steering wheel. In the parts of the country where road crown is more severe, greater caster spread may be necessary.

Suppose that a car owner came to you with the complaint that his car pulled to the right. Upon checking the caster angles, you discovered that the left front wheel had 1/2° positive and the right front wheel had 1° negative. From a wheel alinement viewpoint, do you suppose that you have found the problem? Yes. The car has "opposite" caster readings that will cause a severe pull to the right.

Incorrect caster spread, by itself, will cause a vehicle to pull to one side. However, other causes of *pulling* are: badly worn or scuffed front tires, unequal tire pressures, heavier load on one side, bound or tight idler arm, incorrect settings of other angles, different tire or wheel size on one side.

Fig. 5-14. To measure caster, first turn left front wheel "in" 20° and adjust gauge bubble to read 0°. (Bear Manufacturing Company)

Effects of Too Much POSITIVE Caster

1. Too much positive caster causes hard steering.
2. Too much positive caster causes excessive road shock and shimmy.

Effects of Too Much NEGATIVE Caster

1. Too much negative caster provides for easier steering at low speeds.
2. Too much negative caster causes instability at high speeds.
3. Too much negative caster causes wander and weave.

Effects of UNEQUAL Caster

1. Unequal caster causes the vehicle to pull toward the side of the leading king pin or ball joint.
2. To offset road crown pull, **more** caster, toward positive, is placed on the right wheel.

READING THE CASTER ANGLE

In reading the caster angle using a magnetic-type caster/camber gauge that attaches to the front wheel hub, the following procedures generally apply (always adhere to the individual equipment manufacturer's gauge operating instructions):

1. With the front wheels resting on turning radius gauges in straight ahead position, adjust gauge scales so gauge pointers read zero on both sides of the vehicle.

2. Turn left front wheel in toward center of vehicle until turning radius scale reads 20°. With thumbscrew located under gauge body, adjust *caster* spirit level until bubble reads zero.

Fig. 5-15. Then turn left front wheel "out" 20° (40° swing) and read caster angle. Repeat for right wheel caster. (Bear Manufacturing Company)

3. Turn wheel out from center of vehicle until turning radius scale reads 20° (40° swing). Read left front wheel caster on caster scale located on the right side of the spirit level.

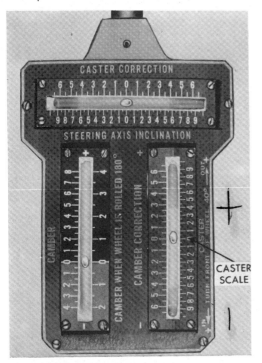

Fig. 5-16. On magnetic caster/camber gauge, caster spirit level and scale are on right side. (Bear Manufacturing Company)

Note: Positive caster is indicated if the bubble lies *toward* the wheel from the zero point on the scale. Negative caster is indicated if bubble lies *away* from the wheel from the zero point on the scale.

4. Repeat same procedure on right front wheel.

INTERPRETING CASTER ANGLE READINGS

Once caster readings are recorded for both front wheels, refer to the car manufacturer's specification sheet for the specified caster "range" for the particular make, model, and year of the vehicle. The car manufacturer does not provide specific and recommended caster readings for left and right front wheels, but rather a range within which to work—a range with very definite minimum and maximum limits. The caster readings of both front wheels must lie within the given range.

For example, for a particular car the caster specification range is 1/2° N–1/2° P. Following Figure 5-17 and re-

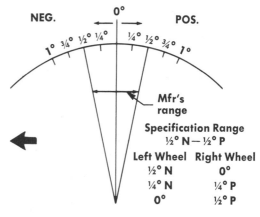

Fig. 5-17. Car manufacturer provides specification range (Ex. 1/2° N–1/2° P) within which both front wheels must be set.

calling the need for 1/2° more caster, toward positive, on the right front wheel to offset road crown, possible correct combinations of left and right wheel settings are presented. (Where preferred settings are specified by the car manufacturer, always adhere to the preferred recommendations.) Oftentimes, it isn't necessary to adjust both front wheels on a job. Let's say that upon checking this car, caster for the left wheel measures 1/4° negative and for the right wheel 3/4° positive. You will note that (1) the right wheel caster lies outside of specifications and (2) the caster spread between the two wheels is greater than 1/2°. Because the left front wheel is within the given specification range in this case, it is only necessary to correct caster on the right wheel.

REVIEW QUIZ

The following quiz is for your review of the Caster angle. Read each question or statement and its several possible answers. Select the answer that best completes the statement or answers the question, and check the answer sheet provided at the end of the text.

1. There are five wheel alinement angles. Which of the following is not one of them?
   a. Caster.
   b. Steering Axis Inclination.
   c. Toe-in.
   d. Turning radius.
   e. Camber.
   f. Toe-out.

2. The term "Wheel Alinement" includes as one common problem a number of factors. Which of the following is not included?
   a. Tire mileage.
   b. Stability.

   c. Steering control.
   d. Braking effort.
   e. Turning effort.

3. The forward or backward tilt of the king pin or ball joint from the vertical line is termed:
   a. Camber.
   b. Caster.
   c. Toe-in.
   d. Steering axis inclination.

4. Caster is:
   a. A toe-in angle.
   b. A tire-wearing angle.
   c. A turning angle.
   d. A directional control angle.

5. Caster is measured in:
   a. Degrees.
   b. Fractions of an inch.
   c. Centimeters.
   d. None of the above.

6. Positive caster is:
   a. The inward tilt of the king pin or ball joint at the top.
   b. The forward tilt of the king pin or ball joint at the top.
   c. The backward tilt of the king pin or ball joint at the top.
   d. None of these.

7. An automobile's tendency to maintain a straight ahead course increases with:
   a. Positive camber.
   b. Negative caster.
   c. Negative camber.
   d. Positive caster.

8. One of the purposes of caster is:
   a. To maintain equal toe-in of the front wheels.
   b. To offset road crown.
   c. To maintain steering wheel in straight ahead position.
   d. To provide easy steering.

9. Negative caster tends to:
    a. Make it more difficult to recover vehicle from turn.
    b. Decrease tire wear on outside edge of tread.
    c. Make the vehicle wander and weave.
    (d.) Make the vehicle easier to steer.

10. Positive caster tends to:
    a. Make the vehicle easier to steer.
    b. Reduce road shock and shimmy.
    (c.) Provide good directional control.
    d. Offset road crown.

11. The influence of positive caster is a tendency for the front wheels to:
    (a.) Toe-in.
    b. Toe-out.
    c. Toe-out on turns.
    d. Toe-in on turns.

12. To read the caster angle, the wheel is:
    a. Placed in straight ahead position.
    b. First turned outward 20°.
    (c.) First turned inward 20°.
    d. Turned through a 50° swing.

13. A negative caster reading indicates:
    a. That the top of the king pin or ball joint is back at the top from the vertical line.
    b. That the top of the king pin or ball joint is inward at the top from the vertical line.
    (c.) That the top of the king pin or ball joint is for-

ward at the top from the vertical line.
    d. That the reading is outside the manufacturer's specification range.

14. If the caster angle is not the same on both front wheels:
    a. No effect is felt in steering.
    b. The vehicle will pull toward the side of greater caster.
    c. The vehicle will pull toward the side of least caster.
    (d.) It creates a tendency for both front tires to wear abnormally.

15. For driving stability at high speeds caster should be set:
    a. Equal on both wheels.
    b. Negative.
    (c.) Positive.
    d. Positive on one wheel.

16. If heavy load is placed in trunk of vehicle, caster setting will:
    a. Move toward negative.
    (b.) Not be affected.
    c. Move toward positive.
    d. Cause easier turning conditions.

17. To correct for road crown pull with caster, we place:
    a. More caster, toward negative, on the right wheel.
    (b.) More caster, toward positive, on the right wheel.
    c. Equal caster on both front wheels.
    d. Positive caster on both front wheels.

18. Caster spread between wheels, for most cars, need not exceed:
    a. 1/4°.
    (b.) 1°.
    c. 3/4°.
    d. 1/2°.

19.   On American cars caster is:
      a. Nonadjustable.
      b. Fixed.
      c. Adjustable.
      d. Automatically estab-
          lished.

20.   If the following caster readings
      were recorded:

          LEFT WHEEL   RIGHT WHEEL
          1 1/2 °N   3/4 °N

      a. The car pulls toward the
          left.
      b. The car travels in straight
          ahead direction without
          pulling to either side.
      c. The car pulls toward the
          right.
      d. The car is within manu-
          facturer's range.

Chapter 6
WHEEL ALINEMENT ANGLES— CAMBER

DEFINITION

The second wheel alinement angle is *Camber*. It is a "tire-wearing" angle. If improperly adjusted away from manufacturer's specifications or away from a particular loading factor of the vehicle, it can cause tires to wear. In addition to being a tire-wearing angle, however, it is also a directional control angle. Its definition is: *Camber is the inward or outward tilt of the wheel at the top.*

Camber is the angle formed between true vertical (0°) and the wheel viewed from the *front* of the vehicle. When the wheel is tilted outward at the top from true vertical (away from the engine), it is known as *Positive Camber*.

When the wheel is tilted inward at the top from true vertical (toward the engine), it is known as *Negative Camber*.

PURPOSE

The Purposes of Camber are:

1. To bring the road contact of the tire more nearly under the point of load.
2. To provide easy steering by having the weight of the vehicle borne by the inner wheel bearing and spindle.

Camber measurements are taken from true vertical and measured in degrees. As with caster, true vertical or 0° is the starting point and the terms "positive" and "negative" denote the position of the angle on either side of zero. The only difference is that for caster, we viewed the position of the spindle support arm from the side of the vehicle, while for camber we view the wheel from the front of the vehicle.

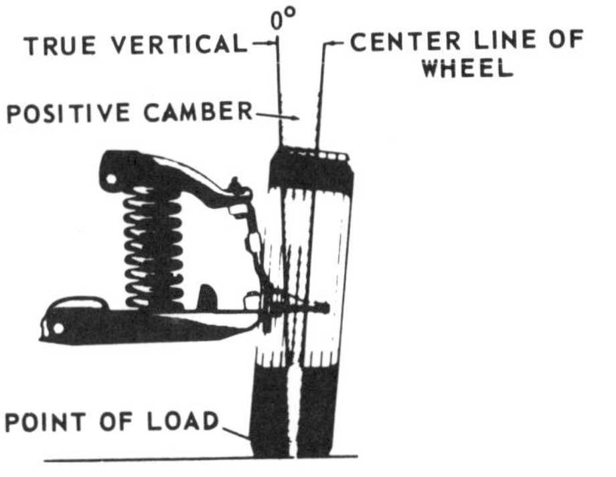

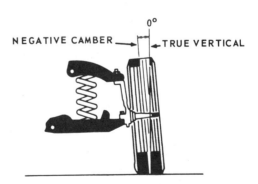

Fig. 6-1. When the wheel is tilted outward at the top from true vertical (0°), it is known as positive camber. (Bear Manufacturing Company)

Fig. 6-2. When the wheel is tilted inward at the top from true vertical (0°), it is known as negative camber. (Bear Manufacturing Company)

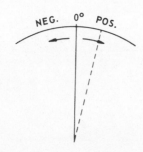

Fig. 6-3. Camber measurements are always taken from true vertical (0°) and measured in degrees. (Bear Manufacturing Company)

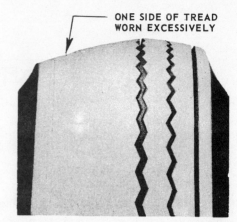

ONE SIDE OF TREAD WORN EXCESSIVELY

Fig. 6-5. Camber wear appears on one side of the tire tread. (Sears, Roebuck and Company)

CAMBER WEAR

Camber is a tire wearing angle because a tilted wheel creates varying diameters of the tire. If the tilt of the wheel is outward at the top, as illustrated, the outside of the tire has a smaller diameter than the inside. Theoretically, as the vehicle rolls down the highway, the smallest diameter slips and slides over the pavement trying to equal the speed of the largest diameter. The outside ribs of the tire tread will wear faster than the inside and cause a smooth-type wear around the entire circumference of the tire.

How does camber become excessive so that it causes tire wear in this manner? There are two reasons:

1. Camber is not adjusted properly to specifications.
2. Unusual loading characteristics of the vehicle cause the camber of the wheels to change. The independent suspension design allows the top of the wheel to move in and out while the bottom of the wheel remains stationary. *Camber changes under weight!*

DIRECTIONAL CONTROL

Camber is also a directional control angle. A tilted wheel will roll around the apex of its cone. The wheel behaves as though it is an ice cream cone. If we lay a cone on a flat surface and tap against the large end, it will roll about its apex.

The same effect takes place with an excessively cambered wheel. With heavy *positive* camber, the wheel will roll outward, away from the car. With heavy *negative* camber, the wheel

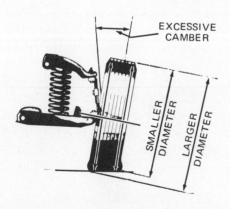

EXCESSIVE CAMBER

SMALLER DIAMETER

LARGER DIAMETER

Fig. 6-4. Excessive camber (Neg. or Pos.) creates varying diameters of the tire. (Bear Manufacturing Company)

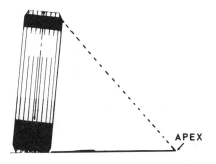

Fig. 6-6. A tilted wheel will roll around the apex of its cone. (Bear Manufacturing Company)

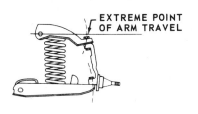

Fig. 6-7. Long and short arm suspension construction allows camber to change under weight distribution. (Bear Manufacturing Company)

will roll inward, toward the center of the car. As we view both front wheels, *the vehicle will pull to the side having the greater camber.* One car manufacturer states that 1/2° difference between the two front wheels will cause a car to pull to one side. Less camber is used on today's car because of:

1. Smaller wheels.
2. Wider tires.
3. Greater speeds.
4. Steering axis inclination or king pin inclination.

Camber Change

As has been stated, camber changes with changed weight because the long and short arm suspension construction allows the top of the wheel to move in and out while the bottom remains stationary to the road surface. At normal riding height, the upper control arm outer end (ball joint) lies slightly downward in its arc of travel, meaning that as the coil spring compresses, the outer end of the control arm rises and the ball joint reaches the extreme *outward* point

of its travel. This increases camber, toward positive. In this way, the driver's weight increases camber on the left wheel. Conversely, the driver's weight causes camber on the right wheel to decrease, toward negative. With the addition of a passenger in the front seat, however, camber of both wheels will return to approximately its original settings.

Camber Pull

If the weight of the driver is excessive or the car is loaded heavily on one side, the vehicle will pull to one side because of camber change. You may have experienced the pull of a vehicle to the right with three people in the car, the heaviest sitting in the right corner of the rear seat. If this person sits instead in the middle or behind the driver, the car will not pull. You can change steering control of the automobile by the shifting of weight, effecting changes in the camber angles.

As a wheel alinement specialist, you must be constantly aware of load or weight distribution when alining cars, especially as it affects camber.

Harmful Effects of INCORRECT Camber

1. Excessive wear on ball joints.
2. Excessive wear on wheel bearings.
3. Excessive wear on one side of tire tread (*Negative Camber*—inside wear; *Positive Camber*—outside wear).
4. Excessive unequal Camber will cause vehicle to pull to one side.

READING THE CAMBER ANGLE

In reading the camber angle with a magnetic-type caster/camber gauge that attaches to the front wheel hub, the following procedures generally apply (always adhere to the individual equipment manufacturer's gauge operating instructions):

1. Place vehicle front wheels on turning radius gauges, wheels straight ahead.
2. Install gauge to one wheel hub in a horizontal plane.
3. Read camber on camber scale

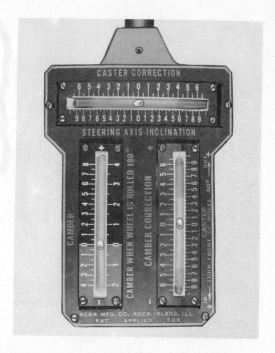

Fig. 6-9. On magnetic caster/camber gauge, camber spirit level and scale are on left side. (Bear Manufacturing Company)

located left of the spirit level bubble, the outer scale.
4. Repeat same procedure on opposite wheel.

Once camber readings are recorded for both front wheels, refer to the car manufacturer's specification for the specified camber range of the particular make, model, and year of vehicle. As for caster, the car manufacturer does not specifically indicate what the camber readings should be for each front wheel, but instead a range is provided within which to work.

Fig. 6-8. To measure camber, place front wheels in straight ahead direction and read the camber angle. (Bear Manufacturing Company)

INTERPRETING CAMBER ANGLE READINGS

For example, one particular car's camber specifications are 1/4° P–1° P,

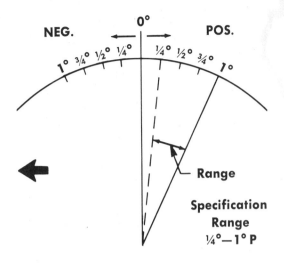

Fig. 6-10. Car manufacturer provides specification range within which both front wheels must rest.

Remember:

1. Camber changes under weight.
2. Camber is a "tire-wearing" angle.
3. Camber is a directional control angle.

CASTER–CAMBER SETTINGS

Caster and Camber angles are so closely interrelated that it is difficult to discuss one without mentioning the other. Both are directional control angles (either one can cause a vehicle to pull to one side), while only one is a tire-wearing angle (camber). Both are affected by changes in weight distribution in the vehicle. For example, with more than the normal load in the trunk:

1. Caster increases, toward positive.
2. Camber of both wheels decreases, toward negative.

Although the car manufacturer provides wheel alinement specifications based upon vehicle "curb weight" (full fuel tank, oil, and water; recommended tire pressures, and at normal riding height within recommended tolerances), the prime consideration for the wheel alinement specialist is, *weight distribution or car loadings for each vehicle* as it affects tire mileage, steering ease, and handling characteristics.

Over the years, car manufacturers and wheel alinement people have modified their thinking in their approach to caster-camber settings and where they should be placed to achieve best results. There are three different current approaches that are worthy of consideration:

with maximum variation between wheels, 1/2°. Following the illustration, the camber range is indicated within which both front wheels must lie. Experience over the years has dictated that for the average wheel alinement job and for the average family car, you can be assured that if camber is set 0°-1/4° P (1/4° P, in this example) *equal on both sides* of the vehicle, good results will be obtained.

LEFT WHEEL   RIGHT WHEEL
1/4° P   1/4° P

For a salesman who is usually alone in the vehicle or for a heavy driver, it is necessary to vary the camber settings to fit the loading characteristics of the vehicle. Perhaps 0°-1/4° N for the left wheel and 1/2° P-3/4° P on the right.

	Group 1		Group 2		Group 3	
	L.W.	R.W.	L.W.	R.W.	L.W.	R.W.
CAMBER	1/2°P	0°	1/4°P	1/4°P	0°	1/2°P
CASTER	0°	0°	1/2°N	0°	1/2°N	0°

Study the three considering:

1. Tire mileage.
2. Steering ease.
3. Car pull to one side and road crown.

We will analyze each group separately.

Group 1

1. Camber compensates for road crown pull (left wheel).
2. Heavy camber on the left wheel will increase further with driver's weight. (Note possible danger of outside tire wear.)
3. Greater camber on the left wheel makes the car easier to steer on left turns; harder on right turns.

Group 2

1. Equal camber assures best tire mileage. Although the driver's weight increases camber on left wheel and decreases it on the right, another passenger (in the front seat) causes camber to return to "equal" original settings.
2. Equal camber assures equal turning effort.
3. Road crown pull is compensated for by the caster angle.

Group 3

1. Greater camber on the right wheel increases the danger of outside tire wear and also the danger of the car pulling to right.
2. Greater camber on the right wheel makes steering easier on right corners; difficult on left.
3. Caster spread may not be great enough to compensate for road crown pull and overcome the camber pull.

It is generally agreed that Group 2 provides best tire mileage, steering ease, and handling. Road crown pull is compensated for by the caster angle.

REVIEW QUIZ

The following quiz is designed to help review your understanding of the Camber angle, its effects and influences. Be selective in your choice; only one answer is correct. Check your answers against the answer sheet at the rear of the text.

1. The inward or outward tilt of the top of the wheel from a vertical plane is termed:
    a. Caster.
    b. Toe-in.
    c. Toe-out on turns.
    d. Camber.
2. Camber is measured in:
    a. Degrees.
    b. Fractions of an inch.
    c. Centimeters.
    d. None of the above.

3. Camber is built into an automobile for the purpose of:
   a. Easier cornering.
   b. Compensating for the loading effect on wheels.
   c. Partially relieving the pressure on springs.
   d. Assisting wheels to maintain a straight ahead course.

4. Positive camber is:
   a. The inward tilt of the king pin or ball joint at the top.
   b. The inward tilt of the wheel at the top.
   c. The outward tilt of the wheel at the top.
   d. None of these.

5. A negatively cambered wheel has the tendency to:
   a. Roll outward, away from the vehicle.
   b. Toe-out.
   c. Toe-in.
   d. Roll inward toward center of vehicle.

6. Camber is primarily a:
   a. Steering angle.
   b. Tire-wearing angle.
   c. Toe-in angle.
   d. None of these.

7. Because camber changes under weight, the most important consideration should be:
   a. Steering stability.
   b. Steering ease.
   c. Tire wear.
   d. Directional control.

8. Excessive positive camber usually causes:
   a. Wear on inside of tire tread.
   b. Wear at center of tire tread.
   c. Wear on outside of tire tread.
   d. No effect on tire wear.

9. If heavy load is placed in trunk of vehicle, camber setting will:
   a. Move toward negative.
   b. Not be affected.
   c. Move toward positive.
   d. Make turning easier.

10. If the camber angle is not the same on both front wheels:
    a. No effect is felt in steering.
    b. Vehicle will pull toward the side of greater camber.
    c. Vehicle will pull toward the side of least camber.
    d. It creates a tendency for both front tires to wear abnormally.

11. Excessive tire wear on inside of tire indicates:
    a. Excessive positive caster.
    b. Excessive positive camber.
    c. Excessive negative camber.
    d. Excessive negative caster.

12. Incorrect camber causes:
    a. Excessive wear to idler arms.
    b. Excessive wear to ball joints.
    c. Excessive wear to spindle.
    d. Excessive wear to steering gear.

13. A heavy driver will cause camber to:
    a. Increase on right side of vehicle.
    b. Decrease on left side of vehicle.

    c. Increase on left side of vehicle.

    d. Effect no change on either side.

14. For the average wheel alinement job, camber spread between wheels:

    a. Need not exceed 1/2°.

    b. Need not exceed 1°.

    c. Need not exceed 3/4°.

    d. Should be equal.

15. Excessive negative camber usually causes:

    a. Wear on inside of tire tread.

    b. Wear at center of tire tread.

    c. Wear at both edges of tire tread.

    d. Wear on outside of tire tread.

16. To read the camber angle, the wheel is:

    a. Turned through a 40° swing.

    b. Turned outward 20°.

    c. Placed in straight ahead position.

    d. Jacked up from turning radius gauges.

17. Camber, for American cars is:

    a. Nonadjustable.

    b. Fixed.

    c. Adjustable.

    d. Automatically established.

18. Car manufacturer's camber specifications are 0°–1° P. For the average job and for best results, settings should be:

    a. Left wheel, 0° P; right wheel, 1° P.

    b. Left wheel, 1/2° P; right wheel, 1° P.

    c. Left wheel, 1/4° P; right wheel, 1/4° P.

    d. Left wheel, 1/2° P; right wheel, 0°.

19. Caster and camber settings are closely interrelated. The problem example below indicates the presence of tire wear. Where will it be found?

LEFT WHEEL	RIGHT WHEEL
Camber 3/4° P	1/4° P
Caster 0°	0°

    a. Inside edge of left front tire.

    b. Outside edge of right front tire.

    c. Inside edge of right front tire.

    d. Outside edge of left front tire.

    e. Both front tires.

20. The above problem would also indicate that the vehicle pulls to one side. In which direction, if any?

    a. Pull toward the right.

    b. Pull toward the left.

    c. Didn't pull in either direction.

Chapter 7
WHEEL ALINEMENT ANGLES—
STEERING AXIS INCLINATION
AND TURNING RADIUS

STEERING AXIS INCLINATION

The third wheel alinement angle is Steering Axis Inclination. It is a directional control angle and is nonadjustable.

DEFINITION

Steering Axis Inclination is the inward tilt of the king pin or ball joint at the top.

Measured in degrees, steering axis inclination is the angle formed between true vertical (0°) and a projected line drawn through the center of the king pin as viewed from the *front* of the vehicle. When the king pin was the most common method of swiveling front wheels, the angle was called *king pin inclination.* Because the king pin arrangement is still in use in trucks, that term remains popular. However, *Steering Axis Inclination* is the more modern

term since it applies to the popular use of ball joints on today's suspension systems. The angle is the same, but instead of a projected line drawn through the king pin, the line is centered through the upper and lower ball joints.

PURPOSE

The purposes of Steering Axis Inclination are:

1. To reduce the need for excessive camber.
2. To distribute the weight of the vehicle more nearly under the road contact of the tire.
3. To provide a pivot point about which the wheel will turn producing easy steering.
4. To aid steering stability.

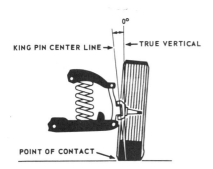

Fig. 7-1. Steering axis inclination is the angle formed between true vertical (0°) and a projected line drawn through center of king pin. (**Bear Manufacturing Company**)

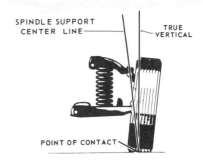

Fig. 7-2. Steering axis inclination is the angle formed between true vertical (0°) and a projected line drawn through the upper and lower ball joints. (**Bear Manufacturing Company**)

POINT OF INTERSECTION

The King Pin Inclination or Steering Axis Inclination projected line, the true vertical line, and the camber projected line all meet at a point that lies below the road surface and to the inside of the tire. This point is called the *point of intersection*. The point of intersection provides a *pivot point* about which the wheel turns. If the wheel were permitted to roll instead of pivot on a turn, the vehicle would be more difficult to steer around a corner and to park. Also, a change in location of this "point" will result in poor directional control. *It will cause a vehicle to steer hard on turns, wander, and pull to one side when traveling in straight ahead direction.* Should the point of intersection rise and change its location (for example, up to the road surface), the deflections of the tire as the vehicle travels down the highway, will cause the "point" to change: first *up*, and then *down*, *below* the road surface. [The deflections of the tire cause a change in rolling radius (diameter) of the wheel and tire assembly.] This causes

the vehicle to wander and will create a "hunting" response to steering.

Therefore, you can see that a bent spindle changes the steering axis inclination angle, thus changing the location of the point of intersection, and in turn causing poor directional control and steering instability. The vehicle will pull to one side because the change in point of intersection causes one wheel to assume a greater directional influence over the other.

DIRECTIONAL CONTROL

The effects of spindle travel created by steering axis inclination are not unlike the effects of positive or negative caster. As the wheels are turned, the rise and fall of the spindle causes the front of the vehicle to rise. Vehicle weight constantly bearing against the spindle ends will automatically force the spindles to return to straight ahead direction. Line B in the illustration traces the travel, on turns, of a spindle, having steering axis inclination with no caster. The spindle acts like a ball in a soup bowl. When released, the ball will work

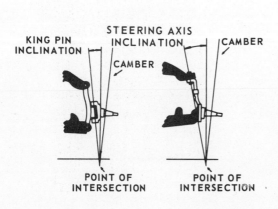
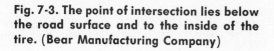

Fig. 7-3. The point of intersection lies below the road surface and to the inside of the tire. (Bear Manufacturing Company)

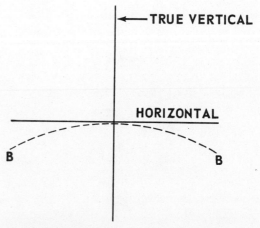

Fig. 7-4. Line B traces the travel of the spindle on turns having steering axis inclination with no caster.

its way, rolling up and down and back and forth inside the bowl until it comes to rest at the bottom—seeking its lowest point. As with an automobile spindle, its lowest point is in straight ahead direction.

In summary, this is an angle that has the same purposes as camber and yet the same directional control factors as caster. Some have wondered, why have this angle? Theoretically the combined angles of camber and caster should take its place. One manufacturer made an attempt at zero (0°) steering axis inclination on both front wheels. The following year the angle was restored to 7°, which demonstrates its necessity and its importance to good directional control.

READING THE STEERING AXIS INCLINATION ANGLE

For an accurate check of the steering axis inclination angle, the recommended procedure is to use a gauge clamp adapter or attach the gauge assembly to the spindle nut. This procedure will eliminate the possibility of "wheel roll," which would interfere with an accurate reading. Even with the brake pedal depressor in position against the foot brake and all four wheels locked, some "wheel roll" takes place on those cars with Bendix brake systems when front wheels are manually turned. That is why manufacturers prefer measuring steering axis inclination from the spindle nut to obtain most accurate readings (always adhere to the individual equipment manufacturer's gauge operating instructions):

1. Place front wheels in straight ahead position. Adjust turning radius gauge scales so gauge pointers read zero.

Fig. 7-5. The steering axis inclination angle is measured from the spindle. (Bear Manufacturing Company)

2. Turn left front wheel IN toward center of vehicle until turning radius scale reads 20°. With thumbscrew, adjust steering axis inclination level until bubble reads zero.

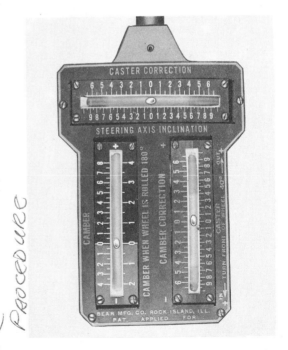

Fig. 7-6. Read bubble on upper scale horizontal to wheel. (Bear Manufacturing Company)

3. Turn wheel OUT from center of vehicle until turning radius scale reads 20° (40° swing). Read steering axis inclination on lower scale of level.

4. Repeat same procedure on right front wheel.

INTERPRETING STEERING AXIS INCLINATION ANGLE READINGS

To properly read steering axis inclination, the camber angle must always be considered. Some manufacturers specify a certain Steering Axis Inclination (S.A.I.) reading at 0° camber; some at 1/2° camber; some at 3/4° camber. To get adjusted reading:

1. *Record* the steering axis inclination reading.
2. *Add* the camber reading, *if positive*, to the S.A.I. reading.
3. *Subtract* the camber reading, *if negative*, from the S.A.I. reading.

For example, assume the manufacturer specifies 7° at 0° camber. Your reading was 6½° at ½° positive camber. Following (2) above, add ½° to the actual reading of 6½°. The total is 7°, the amount the manufacturer specified.

Today very few wheel alinement specialists measure steering axis inclination angles. In fact, some car manufacturers no longer publish a steering axis inclination standard for their vehicles. That is understandable because it is a *nonadjustable* angle and can be corrected only by replacing the spindle support arm (ball joint suspension). Consequently, at the time that wheel alinement angles are being checked, an excessive *camber* reading of 2° to 3°, positive or negative, should alert the wheel alinement specialist to the possibility of a bent spindle. Before checking spindle, be sure, of course, that both upper and lower control arm mountings and control arms are in good condition and securely tightened. Then check the spindle for damage (bent), remove the wheel assembly, attach a dial indicator to the spindle, and slowly rotate it about the spindle. The dial indicator reading should not vary more than five-thousandths (.005) of an inch. Run-out exceeding this amount requires that the spindle and spindle support arm be replaced.

TURNING RADIUS

The next wheel alinement angle is Turning Radius. It is a tire-wearing angle and is nonadjustable.

DEFINITION

Turning radius is: *toe-out on turns*. It means that on every corner, left or right, the fronts of the front wheels are farther apart than the backs of the front wheels. This is called toe-out on turns and is controlled by the angle of the *spindle steering arms*. Turning Radius is often referred to as "steering geometry" because of the angle relationships that the two front wheels assume on cornering or in steering.

Turning Radius and especially the amount of turning radius for a particular vehicle is determined by the wheelbase. Theoretically, a line is projected through the rear end housing and extended outward from the vehicle. With the front wheels turned, in either direction, corresponding lines are drawn from the center of the wheel

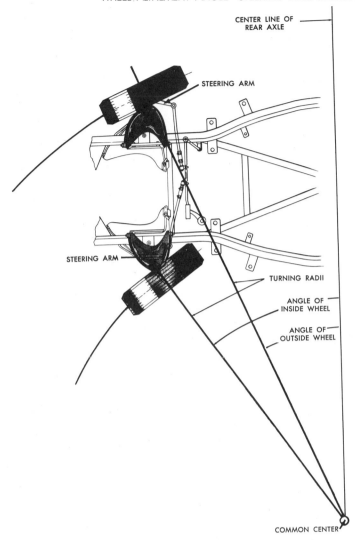

CENTER LINE OF
REAR AXLE

STEERING ARM

STEERING ARM

TURNING RADII

ANGLE OF
INSIDE WHEEL

ANGLE OF
OUTSIDE WHEEL

COMMON CENTER

Fig. 7-7. The front wheels turn about a common center determined by the wheelbase of the vehicle. (Bear Manufacturing Company)

or spindle outward until they meet the projected line of the rear housing. In every instance, you will note, the inside wheel of a corner regardless of direction of turn, creates a larger angle than the outside wheel. This difference in the angles of the two wheels causes the front wheels to assume a toe-out position on turns. This toe-out position aids in steering the vehicle through turns with minimum tire scuff and tire squeal.

PURPOSE

The purpose of turning radius is to reduce scuffing of tires during cornering to a minimum.

Theoretically, whenever wheels and tires are not running parallel to each other, tires will scrape and scuff against the pavement, which causes them to wear excessively. Yet here is an angle that is purposely designed to prevent wheels from running parallel during cornering. But engineers have controlled the turning radius angle through compromise—compromising varying degrees of sharpness of turns against the speed of the vehicle, taking into consideration the car wheelbase. Although the turning radius angle is *not* a perfect angle from a tire-wear standpoint, good results have been achieved. In this regard the wheel alinement specialist looks upon a turning radius reading that differs excessively from recommended specifications, low air pressure, and high rates of speed on cornering as the primary factors causing front tires to wear prematurely.

Toe-out on turns is made possible by angling the steering arms toward the center of the vehicle. Each steering arm has its own arc of travel and, as the front wheels are turned, the outer end of one steering arm will move to a different position in its arc from the other. It is this difference that allows the inside wheel to turn more sharply than the outside wheel.

The illustration shows that the outer end of the steering arm of the inside wheel rests higher in its arc of travel

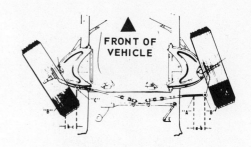

Fig. 7-9. The inside wheel, on a turn, will always turn at a greater angle than the outside wheel. (Bear Manufacturing Company)

(C) than its opposite arm (B). *Note that both arms travel an equal distance when the steering wheel is turned (B–C, A–B).* The same action takes place when turning in the opposite direction. Because of the greater angle of the inside wheel on a turn, the front wheels are in toed-out position. Thus, the definition: *Toe-out on turns.*

Harmful Effects of Incorrect Turning Radius

1. Excessive wear of tires on turns.
2. Tire squeal on turns, even at low speeds.

READING TURNING RADIUS ANGLES

Turning Radius of each front wheel is generally recorded during the caster angle check.

1. Place front wheels in straight ahead position. Adjust both turning radius

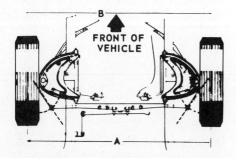

Fig. 7-8. Toe-out on turns is made possible by angling the steering arms in toward the center of the vehicle. (Bear Manufacturing Company)

LEFT FRONT WHEEL

Fig. 7-10. To measure turning radius, turn left front wheel "in" 20°. (Bear Manufacturing Company)

gauge scales to zero. Remove locking pins.

2. Turn left front wheel in toward center of vehicle 20°.

3. Read turning radius gauge scale of *right front wheel* and record.

RIGHT FRONT WHEEL

Fig. 7-11. Read turning radius of right front wheel. (Repeat for left wheel.) (Bear Manufacturing Company)

4. For turning radius reading for *left front wheel*, turn right front wheel in toward center of vehicle 20°. Read turning radius scale on left wheel.

INTERPRETING TURNING RADIUS READINGS

Because on a turn the inner wheel turns at a greater angle than the outside wheel, inner wheel recordings should always be greater than 20°. For example, assume a car manufacturer specifies 24¼°. The specification is based upon the fact that: *When the outer wheel turns 20°, the inner wheel turns 24¼°.*

For this car the inner wheel on a turn, turns 4¼° more than the outer wheel. Allowable tolerances between the front wheels are approximately 1°– 1½°. In the above example, the left wheel indicated 24¼° of turning radius. Suppose upon checking the right wheel, we have a reading of 23°. From this example, turning radius for the vehicle would be within tolerance (1¼°) and no change is required.

Some car manufacturers, however, require a somewhat different procedure for checking turning radius. They say: *When inner wheel turns 20°, outer wheel turns* _____? — 17½°, 18°, 18½°? Following this method, the outer wheel records *less* than the inner wheel. So, although this method of checking differs from the first, the principle of the turning radius remains the same. It's another way of saying that the inside wheel turns at a greater angle than the outside wheel.

To correct turning radius, replace the steering arm which is in error.

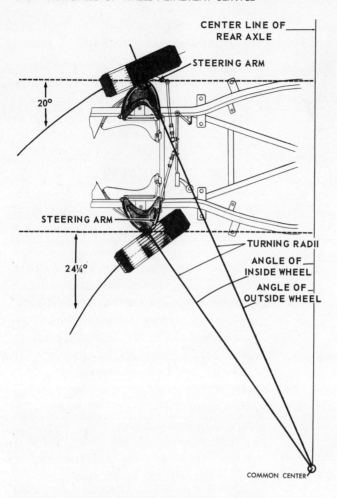

Fig. 7-12. Example: When outer wheel turns 20°, inner wheel turns 24¼°. (Sears, Roebuck and Company)

REVIEW QUIZ

The following quiz reviews the two angles, Steering Axis Inclination and Turning Radius and will test your understanding of their purposes, effects, and influences upon the automobile. Select the answer that best completes each statement and check your choices against the answer sheet at the end of the text.

1. The inward tilt of the king pin or ball joint from the vertical line is termed:
    a. Caster.
    b. Camber.
    c. Steering Axis Inclination.
    d. Turning Radius.

2. Steering Axis Inclination is measured in:
    a. Fractions of an inch.
    b. Centimeters.
    c. Degrees.
    d. None of the above.
3. The steering axis inclination angle is the number of degrees:
    a. That the top of the spindle support arm is tilted toward the center of the vehicle.
    b. Between the spindle support arm and point of intersection.
    c. That the top of the wheel leans outward from the vertical position.
    d. That the top of the spindle support arm is tipped backward or forward from the true vertical position.
4. The purpose of steering axis inclination is:
    a. To offset road crown.
    b. To prevent tire wear.
    c. To reduce the need for excessive camber.
    d. To prevent "shimmy" of the front wheels.
5. Directional stability of a vehicle is established by:
    a. The ratio of the steering gear.
    b. The use of stabilizer bars and sway bars.
    c. Caster angle and steering axis angle.
    d. Camber angle.
6. Incorrect steering axis inclination causes:
    a. Tire wear.
    b. Vehicle to pull to one side.
    c. Shimmy.
    d. Caster change.

7. Steering Axis Inclination provides:
    a. A greater caster effect.
    b. A means of offsetting negative caster.
    c. A pivot point on which the wheel can turn.
    d. Easier removal of the steering knuckle assembly.
8. A vehicle is closer to the road when the front wheels are in a straight ahead position due to:
    a. The angle of the spindle support arms.
    b. The camber angle.
    c. Steering axis inclination.
    d. Toe-in.
9. The point of intersection is:
    a. The point at which the horizontal center line of spindle meets the vertical center line of the spindle support ball joints.
    b. Not affected by any change in the rolling radius of the tire.
    c. Controlled by all factors of alinement.
    d. The point where the center line of the wheel and tire assembly meet the true vertical center line and the center line passing through the ball joints.
10. Steering axis inclination, like turning radius, is:
    a. Self-adjusting.
    b. Nonadjustable.
    c. Adjustable.
    d. Unmeasurable.

11. To read the steering axis inclination angle, the wheel is:
    a. Turned outward 20°.
    b. Placed in straight ahead position.
    c. Turned through a 40° swing.
    d. Rotated 90°.

12. When measuring steering axis inclination, it is necessary to lock the wheel to keep it from turning:
    a. When using equipment that works from the spindle.
    b. When using equipment utilizing a spherical spirit level.
    c. When using equipment that locates from the wheel, tire, or hub.

13. Steering axis inclination may be corrected by:
    a. Adjusting the camber angle.
    b. Adjusting the caster angle.
    c. Replacing the upper ball joints.
    d. Replacing the spindle support arm.

14. The difference in the turning radius between the two front wheels while cornering or making a turn is termed:
    a. Camber.
    b. Toe-in.
    c. Caster.
    d. Toe-out on turns.

15. The purpose of toe-out on turns is to:
    a. Cause the inside wheel to turn at a sharper angle than the outside wheel when turning.
    b. Allow or compensate for normal tolerances in the steering linkage.
    c. Cause both front wheels to turn at the same angle when turning.
    d. Cause the outside wheel to turn at a sharper angle than the inside wheel when turning.

16. Toe-out on turns is controlled by the:
    a. Combined angle.
    b. Length of the tie rod.
    c. Angle of steering arm only.
    d. Length of and angle of steering arm.

17. Incorrect turning radius causes:
    a. Camber change.
    b. Loss of directional control.
    c. Tire wear.
    d. Pull to one side.
18. To read the turning radius angle:
    a. The wheel is turned inward 20°, and reading is taken on opposite wheel.
    b. Both wheels are turned 20° together.
    c. The wheel is turned inward 24¼°, and reading is taken on opposite wheel.
    d. Turning radius is recorded with wheels in straight ahead position.
19. Turning radius may be corrected by:
    a. Adjusting the toe-in angle.
    b. Replacing the spindle support arms.
    c. Replacing the steering arms.
    d. Changing the lower ball joints.
20. Toe-out on turns is created by having:
    a. The spindle support arms tilted backward.
    b. The spindle support arms parallel.
    c. The distance between the ends of the spindle steering arms greater than the distance between the vertical center lines of the ball joints.
    d. A shorter distance between the ends of the spindle steering arms than the distance between the center lines of the spindle ball joints.

Chapter 8
WHEEL ALINEMENT ANGLES— TOE-IN

The fifth and last wheel alinement angle is *toe-in*. It is a tire-wearing angle, and from the standpoint of tire mileage, it is the most critical. Ninety percent of all tire wear complaints may be attributed to incorrect toe-in.

DEFINITION

Toe-in is the difference in distance between the front and rear of the front wheels.

When the fronts of the wheels (line B) are closer together than the backs of the wheels (line A), they are said to have toe-in. It is perhaps the easiest angle to understand and the easiest to adjust on the vehicle. It is also the last

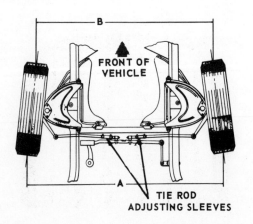

Fig. 8-1. Toe-in is when the fronts of the wheels (line B) are closer together than the backs of the wheels (line A). (Bear Manufacturing Company)

angle to adjust, completing the wheel alinement job.

PURPOSE

The purpose of toe-in is to compensate for widened tolerances in the steering linkage. As a vehicle moves down the highway, the front wheels have a tendency to move outward, absorbing the normal tolerances built into the tie-rod ends, relay rods, and idler arms. Ideal toe-in with the vehicle in motion is "zero" toe. Therefore, to obtain zero toe on the highway, all car manufacturers recommend a toe-in setting when the vehicle is stationary.

At one time, early theorists believed that toe-in was needed to offset camber. It was reasoned that because positive camber causes wheels to roll outward, toe-in was needed to maintain the wheels in straight ahead direction; therefore, the greater the camber, the greater the toe-in required. This is not necessarily so. In recent years with the advent of wider tires and smaller wheels, with less positive camber needed, the more acceptable reasoning for front wheel toe-in has been that relating to the steering linkage. Even today with the wide oval tires and at 0° camber, we have specifications of 1/16", 1/8", and 7/16" toe-in.

When the fronts of the wheels (line B) are farther apart than the backs of the wheels (line A), they are said to have toe-out.

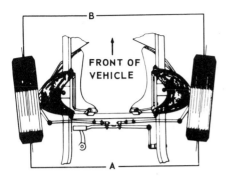

Fig. 8-2. Toe-out is when the fronts of the wheels (line B) are farther apart than the backs of the wheels (line A). (Bear Manufacturing Company)

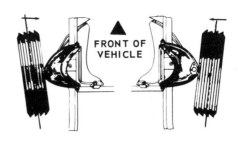

Fig. 8-4. Excessive toe-out wear (scuff) can be felt by passing the hand across the tire from the outside toward the inside. (Bear Manufacturing Company)

TIRE WEAR

A feather edge due to scuffing can be felt by passing the hand across the tire from the inside *toward the outside.* (This is caused by excessive toe-in.)

A feather edge due to scuffing can be felt by passing the hand across the tire from the outside *toward the inside.* (This is caused by excessive toe-out.)

Excessive wear across the tire tread is the most harmful effect of incorrect toe.

Excessive toe-in or toe-out tire wear creates a feather edge across *both* front tires. It is easy to recognize because it looks as though a file has been rubbed across the tire tread. When toe is excessive, tire wear may be detected after less than 200 miles of highway driving.

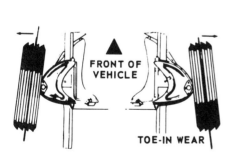

Fig. 8-3. Excessive toe-in wear (scuff) can be felt by passing the hand across the tire from the inside toward the outside. (Bear Manufacturing Company)

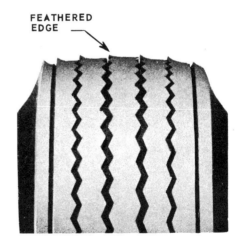

Fig. 8-5. Excessive toe wear causes feather edge to appear on tire tread. (Sears, Roebuck and Company)

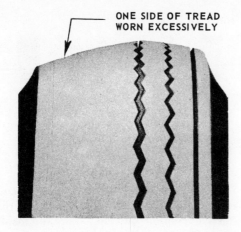

ONE SIDE OF TREAD
WORN EXCESSIVELY

Fig. 8-6. Slight misalinement of toe causes smooth wear on one side of tire tread. (Sears, Roebuck and Company)

Wear from incorrect toe often will appear not as feather edges across the complete tire tread but as smooth, camber-type wear, appearing on only one side of the tire tread *and* occurring on only one wheel. This type of wear is caused by incorrect toe that is *not* excessive, but is only slightly more or slightly less than the car manufacturer's specifications.

Some authorities feel that this occurrence of toe-in wear on one wheel only is caused by the influence of road crown. With slightly heavy toe-in setting, the influence of toe-in is directed toward the outside wheel (right front), causing tire wear to show on the outside of the tire tread. In the same way, a slightly heavy toe-out setting causes the left front tire to wear on the inside.

Rule: (1) A little too much toe-in causes wear on outside of right front tire.

(2) A little too much toe-out causes wear on inside of left front tire.

It is a good rule to remember because many have been fooled into thinking that what looked like camber wear was actually toe-in wear. Therefore, don't make a hasty diagnosis. Always check the vehicle first.

READING THE TOE-IN ANGLE

Three basic methods of measuring toe-in are widely employed today. One uses a toe gauge that physically measures the distance between the two front wheels with the vehicle stationary. Popularly called the "scribe line" method, its measurements are in inches. The second uses a scuff gauge. It requires that the vehicle be driven across a pair of knife-edge blades set in a platform on the floor. Readings are recorded in "feet per mile scuff." The third method involves projecting a toe scale image onto a screen by means of a beam of light. The instrument is called the Projectoe gauge. All three methods involve the use of equipment that is specifically designed for the measuring of the toe-in angle only, as distinct from some deluxe wheel alinement models that measure other angles as well.

Scribe Line Method

To measure toe-in mechanically in this method, a Tire Scriber is used to scribe a line about the circumference of the tire, as illustrated in Figure 8-7. This line or marking on the tire establishes the center line of the tire and wheel assembly, eliminating any influence from a possible bent wheel or tire run-out.

Then the toe-in gauge is placed first at the rear of the front wheels with each pointer directly centered on the

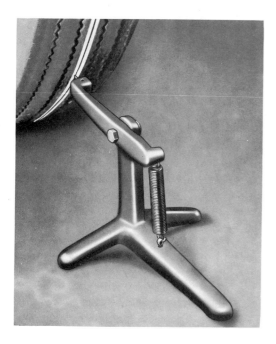

Fig. 8-7. A tire scriber Is used to scribe a line about the circumference of the tire. (**Bear Manufacturing Company**)

Scuff Gauge

To measure toe-in with the Scuff Gauge:

1. Drive vehicle slowly up to tester as straight as possible.
2. With hands off steering wheel, drive slowly across the scuff gauge.

The reading obtained indicates the combined toe-in of both front wheels in feet per mile scuff. For best tire mileage, a toe-in of 0–3 ft per mile scuff is recommended for both passenger cars and trucks.

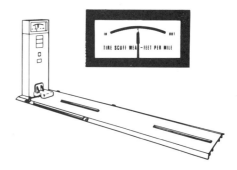

Fig. 8-9. Bear Alinement Tester is calibrated to measure toe in feet per mile scuff. (**Bear Manufacturing Company**)

scribe line on each tire. Then move the gauge into position at the front of the wheels, placing the upright pointer on the scribed center line of the right front tire. The indicator, on the left wheel, will show the exact amount of toe-in or toe-out.

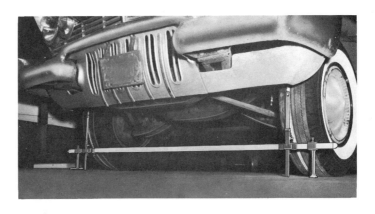

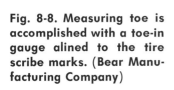

Fig. 8-8. Measuring toe is accomplished with a toe-in gauge alined to the tire scribe marks. (**Bear Manufacturing Company**)

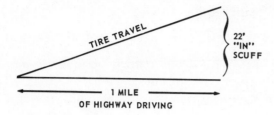

Fig. 8-10. Feet per mile scuff means that for each mile the vehicle is driven, the tires are scuffing sideways the amount recorded.

"Feet per mile scuff" means that for each mile the vehicle is driven, the tires are scuffing sideways the amount recorded. Following the illustration in Figure 8-10, this particular vehicle is dragging or scuffing the front tires 22 feet for every mile it is being driven. Because it is a *toe-in* recording, tire wear will show first at the outside of the right front tire. If it were a toe-out reading, tire wear would show first at the inside of the left front tire.

Guide rules when setting toe-in are:

1/16" toe-in = 11 ft per mile scuff
1/4 turn of tie-rod
adjusting sleeve
= 11 ft per mile scuff

Projectoe

The Projectoe instrument consists of two screens, one for each wheel, upon which the toe scale image is "pro-

Fig. 8-11. One gauge (Projectoe) measures toe by means of a beam of light projected onto a screen. (Bear Manufacturing Company)

Fig. 8-12. A steering wheel holder maintains steering wheel center position while toe is adjusted. (Bear Manufacturing Company)

jected" from a unit on the opposite wheel. Cross projections permit reading the toe position of each wheel with respect to the other wheel. The combined readings from both screens give the total toe-in or toe-out of the vehicle. (Each screen should show one-half of the required toe-in specification.) Each mark on the projected image is one-sixteenth of an inch (1/16"). To operate the Projectoe unit:

1. First, center steering wheel in straight ahead position and install a steering wheel holder. Then, spread the front of the front wheels by pushing lightly outward on both wheels simultaneously.
2. Install the Projectoe units to the front wheels; plug into 110 volt AC outlet; level both units; and focus image on each screen.
3. Adjust tie rod adjusting sleeves until each screen indicates one-half the required toe-in specification. For example, if the specification requires 1/8" toe-in, each wheel should read 1/16" toe-in.

Toe-in is adjusted by turning the tie rod adjusting sleeves (A) equally. Generally, manufacturer's specifications for cars have a range of 0–1/8" toe-in with the average approximately 1/16", and for trucks 0–1/4" toe-in.

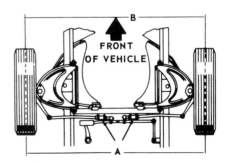

Fig. 8-13. Toe-in is adjusted by turning the tie rod adjusting sleeves equally. (Bear Manufacturing Company)

TOE CHANGE

"Toe change" is a term commonly used to describe a change that occurs in the toe-in angle when load is added to the vehicle or whenever the front springs compress and rebound as from braking (stopping at stop signs, traffic lights) or as the vehicle travels over normal road irregularities. We know that camber changes when the vehicle is in motion (top of the wheel moves in and out; bottom remains stationary) because of the basic design of the independent suspension. However, toe-in, the most critical tire-wearing angle *must not change* under any circumstances, regardless of load, if maximum tire mileage is to be obtained.

"Toe change" occurs whenever the tie rods do not lie in the same plane as the lower control arms. As the front wheels move up and down over road irregularities, tie rod up-and-down movement creates an arc of travel from its inner pivot point that differs from that of the lower control arm. Depending upon the mislocation of its pivot point, it causes the rear of the front wheel either to "pull in" or to "push out," changing the distance between the front of the wheels and upsetting the original toe-in reading at curb weight and at curb riding height. To inspect for suspected "toe change," drive vehicle across scuff gauge with an additional passenger in the front seat or riding on a front fender, and note any change in toe-in reading from that of the driver's weight alone. This duplicates highway driving conditions. If a mechanical toe-in gauge is used, pull down on the front bumper and note any changes in toe-in readings.

"Toe change" is nonadjustable. If it is discovered, adjust toe-in at a setting midway between readings for vehicle empty and vehicle with load.

REVIEW QUIZ

The following quiz is for your review of the toe-in angle. Read each question or statement and its several possible answers. Select the answer that best completes the statement and check against the answer sheet provided at the end of the text.

1. The difference in distance between the wheel centers at the rear of the front tires and the wheel centers at the front of the tires is termed:
    a. Toe-out on turns.
    b. Toe-in or toe-out.
    c. Caster.
    d. Camber.
2. The purpose of toe-in is to:
    a. Ensure that both front wheels are turning about a common pivot.
    b. Ensure that the inside wheel turns at a sharper angle than the outside wheel when turning.
    c. Allow or compensate for normal tolerances in steering linkage.
    d. Ensure that the outside wheel turns at a sharper angle than the inside wheel when turning.
3. Toe-in is a:
    a. Directional control angle.
    b. Tire-wearing angle.
    c. Steering angle.
    d. Turning angle.
4. A worn idler arm affects:
    a. Caster.
    b. Camber
    c. Steering axis inclination.
    d. Toe-in position.

5. Excessive toe-in usually causes:
    a. Excessive tire wear.
    b. Caster misalinement.
    c. Steering gear wear.
    d. Camber misalinement.
6. Toe-in is measured in:
    a. Fractions of an inch.
    b. Degrees.
    c. Centimeters
    d. None of the above.
7. Abnormally fast wear of the entire tire tread usually indicates:
    a. Caster misalinement.
    b. Camber misalinement.
    c. Improper toe-in.
    d. Loose steering gear assembly.
8. A little too much toe-in results in:
    a. Wear on inside of left front tire.
    b. Wear on outside of right front tire.
    c. Wear on outside of both front tires.
    d. Damage to center of tire tread.
9. Any toe-in during vehicle operation will:
    a. Cause hard steering.
    b. Offset the combined angle.
    c. Eliminate directional stability.
    d. Result in needless tire wear.
10. Toe-in of the front wheels is adjustable by:
    a. Lengthening of the drag link.
    b. Bending the spindle steering arms.
    c. Shortening the drag link.
    d. Lengthening or shortening the tie rods.

11. On a front tire, the presence of a feather edge on the tire tread ribs toward the center of the vehicle indicates.
    a. Excessive caster.
    b. Too much toe-in.
    c. Insufficient toe.
    d. Tight front wheel bearings.

12. Tire wear is not caused by:
    a. Excessive toe-in.
    b. Excessive toe-out.
    c. Caster angle set incorrectly.
    d. A bent frame.

13. Toe-in is generally checked by a:
    a. Toe gauge.
    b. Caster/camber gauge.
    c. Spirit level.
    d. Tracking gauge.

14. Toe-in is the:
    a. First angle to adjust on a wheel alinement job.
    b. Last angle to adjust.
    c. Second angle to adjust, following caster correction.
    d. Only angle to adjust.

15. Average toe-in setting for passenger cars is:
    a. 1/4".
    b. 0".
    c. 1/16".
    d. 1/8".

16. The drive-over type of alinement gauge measures toe-in in:
    a. Fractions of an inch.
    b. Feet per mile scuff.
    c. Inches of wheel roll.
    d. Amount of vehicle travel.

17. "Toe Change," a relatively new term in wheel alinement, describes the change in toe-in:
    a. Caused by the flexing and bending of the tie rods under vehicle operation.
    b. Caused by turning right or left corners.
    c. Caused by changed weight distribution in the vehicle.
    d. Caused by bent and out-of-round wheels.

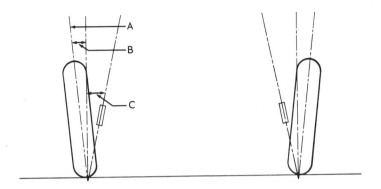

Fig. 8-14. Wheel alinement angles.

18. B is the:
    a. Caster angle.
    b. Point of intersection.
    c. Camber angle.
    d. Steering axis inclination
        angle.

19. A is the:
    a. True vertical line.
    b. Steering axis center line.

    c. Camber angle.
    d. Camber center line.

20. C is the:
    a. Point of intersection.
    b. Steering axis inclination
        angle.
    c. Caster angle.
    d. Toe-in angle.

SUMMARIZING THE WHEEL ALINEMENT ANGLES

Angle	Purpose	Too Much Causes
CASTER, POSITIVE	Directional stability for straight ahead driving, out of a turn- Point of Load ahead of tire contact. Compensates for road crown (unequal).	Hard steering, road shock. Low-speed shimmy.
CASTER, NEGATIVE	Easy steering at slow speeds, easy vehicle parking—Point of Load behind tire contact. Compensates for road crown (unequal).	Touchy steering at high speeds. Wander and Weave. Road shock.
CAMBER	Places point of vehicle load under tire contact. Steering ease. Prevent rapid tire wear.	POSITIVE Tire wear on outside ribs of tire tread. Wear on ball joints and wheel bearings.
STEERING AXIS INCLINATION	Directional stability, turning ease at low speed, reduce need for greater camber. Places point of load under tire contact.	Excessive Camber. Wheel bearing failure. Bent spindle—.005" run-out tolerance.

Too Little Causes	Unequal Causes	Illustrations
Less steering stability for straight ahead driving, less steering wheel "returnability," out of a turn.	Pull to side of least positive caster. Excessive, unequal brake action.	SHOULDER WEAR
Harder steering. Less steering wheel "returnability."	Pull to side of greater negative caster. Excessive unequal brake action.	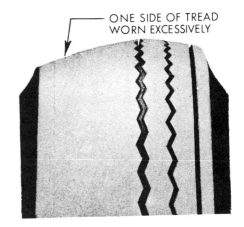

Fig. 8-15. Underinflation wear. (Sears, Roebuck and Company)

NEGATIVE Tire wear on inside ribs of tire tread. Wear on ball joints and wheel bearings.	Pull to side of greater camber. Hard steering on turns.	ONE SIDE OF TREAD WORN EXCESSIVELY
Excessive Camber. Wheel bearing failure. Bent spindle—.005" run-out tolerance	Pull to one side. Wander and weave. Hard steering.	Fig. 8-16. Camber wear. (Sears, Roebuck and Company)

SUMMARIZING THE WHEEL ALINEMENT ANGLES (continued)

Angle	Purpose	Too Much Causes
TURNING RADIUS	Toe-out on turns. Reduces scuffing of tires during cornering to minimum.	Tire squeal on turns. Rapid tire wear.
TOE-IN	Keep wheels parallel when moving by compensating for widened tolerances in steering linkage.	TOE-IN Rapid tire wear. Wear more apparent on outside of right front tire.

Too Little Causes	Unequal Causes	Illustrations

Tire squeal on turns. Rapid tire wear

Tire wear, beyond 1½°–2° tolerance.

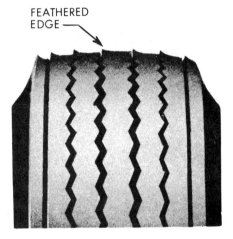

Fig. 8-17. Toe wear. (Sears, Roebuck and Company)

TOE-OUT

Rapid tire wear. Wear more apparent on inside of left front tire.

Could result in steering wheel position off center for straight ahead driving.

Fig. 8-18. Overinflation wear. (Sears, Roebuck and Company)

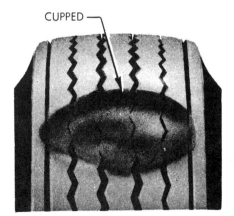

Fig. 8-19. Multi-problem wear. (Sears, Roebuck and Company)

Chapter 9
COMPLETING THE WHEEL ALINEMENT SERVICE

There are two final steps remaining to complete the wheel alinement service.

They are wheel bearing services and front wheel alinement corrections.

STEERING ALINEMENT INSPECTION REPORT

Name_____ _____19_____

Address_____ License No._____ Speedometer_____

Phone_____ Make_____ Body Type_____ Year and Model_____

Inspection and checks made with Bear Precision Gauges and all corrections are made with Bear Equipment.

			LEFT FRONT		RIGHT FRONT		LEFT REAR		RIGHT REAR	
			OK	Not OK	OK	Not OK	OK	Not OK	OK	Not OK
Tire Condition										
Air Pressure in Tires										
Wheel Balance (All)										
Wheel Bent or Eccentric										
Wheel Bearings										
Shock Absorbers										

STEERING GEAR	Adjust	Overhaul	LEFT		RIGHT			LEFT		RIGHT	
			OK	Not OK	OK	Not OK		OK	Not OK	OK	Not OK
Torsion Bar Height							Upper Inner Shaft and Bushings				
Spring Sag or broken							Lower Inner Shaft and Bushings				
Drag Link							Spindle Supports				
Tie Rod Ends							King Pins				
Idler Arm							Upper Outer Pins and Bushings				
Ball Joint Upper							Lower Outer Pins and Bushings				
Ball Joint Lower							Spindle Limit (.005)				

FRONT ALINEMENT CHECK				FACTORY STANDARD	REAR HOUSING CHECK	
Toe-in	IN		OUT			
Camber	Left	•	Right			
Caster	Left	•	Right			
Turning Radius	Left	•	Right			
King Pin Indication	Left	•	Right			

Fig. 9-1. Steering Alinement Inspection Report. (Bear Manufacturing Company)

All operations up to this point—inspecting the front end, steering and suspension parts replacements, steering gear adjustments, and wheel balancing—have been on-the-job preparatory steps that precede wheel alinement corrections. Any attempt to align the front wheels of any vehicle without first checking and correcting other suspension faults will not guarantee customer satisfaction nor provide, necessarily, a safe operating automobile.

WHEEL BEARING SERVICES

Front wheel bearings, their condition and adjustments, are as much the "heart" of the wheel alinement job as is the steering gear. Yet, they are the most neglected items among wheel alinement specialists, generally, because their importance is overlooked. Many wheel alinement jobs have proved unsatisfactory because of loose wheel bearings.

Bearings that are pitted, scored, or loose cause cuppy tire wear, which appears as gouges, intermittently spaced around the tire tread. The cuppy wear becomes more noticeable and more severe as one fault combines with another, such as: dead or weak shock absorbers, underinflated tires, and unbalanced wheels.

Loose wheel bearings also cause the vehicle to wander and weave down the highway. And when wheel bearings are loose, caster, camber, and toe settings cannot be maintained. This not only results in poorer steering control but also causes the cuppy or uneven wear to appear on the inside or outside ribs of the tire tread.

Replacements

Always replace defective wheel bearings! Always adjust loose wheel bearings before setting wheel alinement angles!

Ball bearings and tapered roller bearings are used on today's cars. Each wheel assembly has two bearings —one inner and one outer bearing with the inner bearing being the larger of the two. A tapered roller bearing assembly, shown in Figure 9-3, consists of a bearing and a bearing cup. A grease seal is installed at the inner hub. When removing and installing bearings:

1. Make certain the bearings are not dropped on the floor.
2. Keep bearings clean. Dirt is the cause of most bearing failures. Upon removal, wrap the bearing assemblies in paper.
3. Never drag wheel over spindle.
4. Replace worn or defective grease seals.
5. If compressed air is used to dry the bearings, do not dry the bearings by spinning them.
6. Use new cotter pins.

Fig. 9-2. A front wheel bearing.

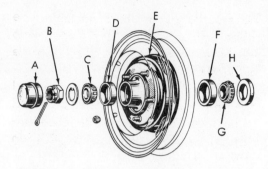

A   Grease cap
B   Adjusting nut
C   Outer wheel bearing
D   Outer bearing cup
E   Hub and drum
F   Inner bearing cup
G   Inner wheel bearing
H   Grease retainer

Fig. 9-3. Exploded view of front wheel bearing assemblies.

Adjustments

A check for bearing roughness is made by spinning the wheel either with a wheel spinner or by hand and placing a hand on the bumper. Roughness felt on the bumper indicates worn or pitted bearings. Replace them if needed.

Bearing looseness is checked by rocking the wheel with one hand at the top of the tire and the other at the bottom. To avoid confusing worn ball joints, king pins, or pins, and bushings with loose wheel bearings, check for movement between the spindle and hub, or between the brake backing plate and drum. Looseness at these points indicates the need for bearing adjustments. When adjusting front wheel bearings, remember that wheel bearings must NOT have free play that can be felt and the wheel must rotate without drag or bind. Drag may be caused by dragging brakes, out-of-round brake drums, loose backing plates, defective bearings, defective cups, or a newly installed grease seal.

The Torque wrench and the car manufacturer's torquing procedures are the accepted means for adjusting front wheel bearings properly. It represents a professional, scientific method of adjustment and with increasing use of front wheel disc brake systems, the torque wrench becomes the only acceptable standard. Always check the car manufacturer's specifications for correct tolerances.

If you do not have a torque wrench, follow this procedure to adjust front wheel bearings safely without a torque wrench:

STEP 1

Remove the cotter pin and tighten the spindle nut using water pump pliers (channel-lock pliers) or 8" crescent wrench to "snug" (approximately 7 ft-lb), while the wheel is rotating. *Check for looseness and wheel drag.* No apparent looseness should be felt.

STEP 2

Insert and lock the cotter pins. If the dust cap contains a static collector, clip the leg of the cotter pin to prevent interference.

WHEEL ALINEMENT EQUIPMENT

Means for adjusting wheel alinement angles and restoring them to original car manufacturer's specification ranges are provided on all American-made cars. The "adjustable" angles are caster, camber, and toe-in. The "nonadjustable" angles are steering axis inclination and turning radius, which can be restored only by the replacement of bent parts.

Wheel alinement equipment is needed to measure these angles, which once adjusted to desired settings, will provide maximum tire mileage and handling ease for all vehicles. Neither replacement of worn steering and suspension parts nor the replacement of worn tires will assure good vehicle performance or front end part longevity without some means for setting wheels in their proper tire-road relationship. Therefore, wheel alinement service, once again, involves front end part replacement services as well as wheel "adjustment" services. One does not stand independently of the other.

There are many kinds of wheel alinement equipment available on the American market. Equipment differs in size, design, and engineering approach to the method of measuring alinement angles. These differences are also apparent as this equipment best fits a particular service application. For example, a body-frame shop that plans to add wheel alinement equipment later to complement its body-frame straightening equipment, will not necessarily purchase a portable-type wheel aliner initially. An owner who leases a service facility may not be allowed to have a pit-type installation— one that would require placing a wheel alinement service in a pit, at floor level. Differences then, primarily are considered in the particular application in which it will be used.

An attempt is made here to divide wheel alinement equipment into two categories, *racks* and *gauges*. Racks determine the working area and the manner in which the vehicle is placed on a level surface as well as the working height involved and amount of space available for wheel alinement operations. Gauges determine the method of measuring wheel alinement angles —spirit level, light projection, electronic, or sight. Each type of equipment has features or advantages that make one or another combination of equipment more suitable for a particular business operation.

Fig. 9-4. Portable type of wheel alinement equipment. (Bear Manufacturing Company)

Racks

There are four basic "rack" approaches to wheel alignment:

1. Portable.
2. Half-rack or stub (pit).
3. Full-length rack (floor or pit).
4. Power rack.

PORTABLE TYPE

Portable equipment features the ability to perform wheel alinement adjustments anywhere inside or outside a service area. Some utilize small stands upon which the vehicle rests to provide working height or higher stands to be

Fig. 9-5. Portable type of wheel alinement equipment (floor model). (Stewart Warner Alemite Division)

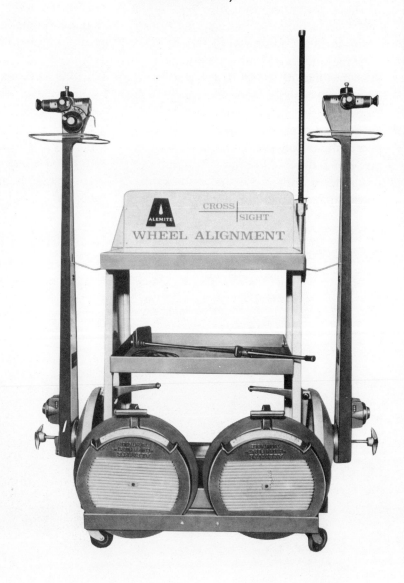

used in conjunction with standard automotive hoists.

Some portable equipment comes in floor models, as illustrated, where the front wheels of the car rest on turning radius gauges placed on the floor.

HALF-RACK OR STUB TYPE (PIT INSTALLATION)

Half-racks or Stub racks require a pit installation and feature the ability to place the vehicle in a work area without jacking, lifting, or driving up runways. Since only one-half a rack is used floor space is saved.

FULL-LENGTH RACKS (FLOOR OR PIT INSTALLATIONS)

Full-length racks are generally placed in a service bay area, or under a canopy in southern climates, and are simply leveled and anchored to the floor. They predetermine vehicle working height, and like portable equipment may be relocated in the service facility without disrupting floor plans.

POWER RACK

The Power Rack is a floor installation unit featuring power-operated runways. Once the vehicle is driven upon it, the runways are raised to a level position. The principal advantage is that the rack length is approximately the same length as the vehicle, eliminating the need for other runways or runway extensions.

Gauges

There are four basic gauges or instruments used to measure wheel alinement angles. Each is accurate and may be adapted to any type of rack installation to provide a desired rack–gauge combination. In every instance, the use of these gauges requires strict adher-

Fig. 9-6. Half-rack or stub rack type of wheel alinement equipment. (Bear Manufacturing Company)

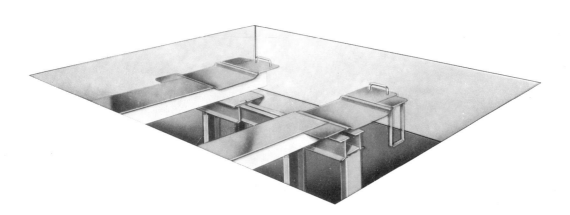

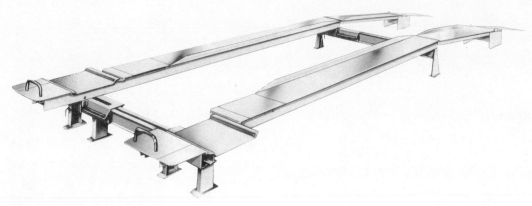

Fig. 9-7. Full rack type of wheel alinement equipment. (Bear Manufacturing Company)

ence to the equipment makers' procedures. Gauge types are:

1. Cross sight.
2. Spirit level.
3. Light projection.
4. Electronic transfer.

CROSS SIGHT

The cross sight gauge attaches to the front wheels and utilizes optical type instruments for measuring alinement angles.

SPIRIT LEVEL

Spirit level or bubble-type gauges are available in various designs. Shown

Fig. 9-8. Power rack type of wheel alinement equipment. (Bear Manufacturing Company)

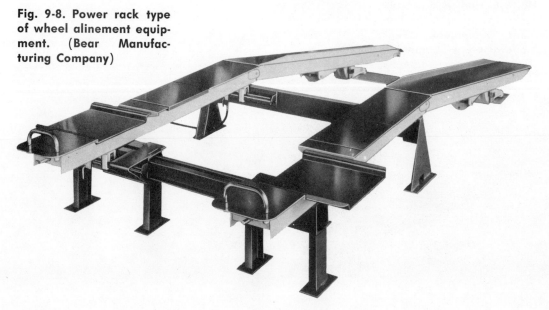

Fig. 9-9. Power rack type of wheel alinement equipment. (Hunter Engineering Company)

here is a magnetic spindle gauge that attaches to the wheel hub. Alinement degree readings are scaled to bubble movement on a dial.

Fig. 9-10. Cross sight type of wheel alinement gauge. (Stewart Warner Alemite Division)

LIGHT PROJECTION

Light projection gauges utilize a screen or target placed in front of the vehicle. Light bulbs project wheel alinement readings from the wheel onto the screen.

ELECTRONIC TRANSFER

The electronic transfer gauges also utilize a screen or target placed in front of the vehicle. In this case the screen is

Fig. 9-11. Spirit level type of wheel aline-ment gauge. (Bear Manufacturing Company)

graduated. Wheel alinement readings are obtained at the wheel and are transferred, electrically, to the screen.

Fig. 9-12. Light projection type of wheel alinement gauge. (Hunter Engineering Company)

WHEEL ALINEMENT CORRECTIONS

Procedure

Because all wheel alinement angles are interrelated, one affecting the other, the following sequence of adjustments is suggested as a guide for all vehicles, regardless of type of suspension.

1. Correct caster.
2. Correct camber.
3. Locate steering wheel in straight ahead position (Hi-Point) and adjust tie rods so wheels are straight ahead.
4. Adjust toe-in.

Adjustment means vary from vehicle to vehicle and often even from year to year of the same make car. For specific adjustment locations and procedures always refer to service manuals provided by the car manufacturer.

Fig. 9-13. Electronic transfer type of wheel alinement gauge. (Bear Manufacturing Company)

Caster—Camber Adjustments

Regardless of the adjustment means or locations, the main consideration *always* is the positioning of the top of the spindle support arm (upper ball joint) in relation to the lower. Whenever a change is contemplated, the *first* consideration is: In which direction should the top of the spindle support arm be moved to achieve the desired results?

EXAMPLE

If in adjusting caster we pivot the entire upper control arm so that the upper ball joint changes its position toward the rear of the car, caster is changed in a *positive direction*. Vice versa, if we pivot the upper control arm so that the upper ball joint moves toward the front of the car, caster is changed in a *negative direction*.

In adjusting camber, always think of the top of the wheel or the upper ball joint and the desired direction of movement. In this example *positive direction* is obtained by moving the entire upper control arm assembly outward, away from the engine. *Negative direction* is obtained by moving the control arm assembly *in* toward the engine.

SHIM ADJUSTMENTS

In the shim method, caster adjustments are made by loosening the upper control arm attaching bolts and repositioning the inner shaft. The upper ball

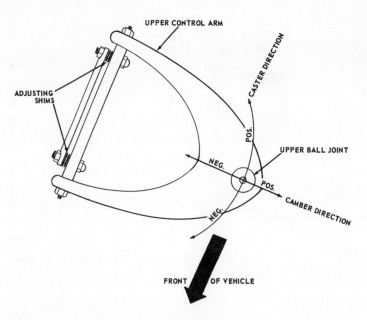

UPPER CONTROL ARM

CASTER DIRECTION

ADJUSTING SHIMS

POS.

NEG.

POS.

UPPER BALL JOINT

CAMBER DIRECTION

NEG.

FRONT OF VEHICLE

Fig. 9-14. An illustration depicting positive and negative directional movement of upper control arm when adjusting caster/camber angles. (Sears, Roebuck and Company)

Fig. 9-15. Upper control arm mounting showing location of caster and camber shims. (Bear Manufacturing Company)

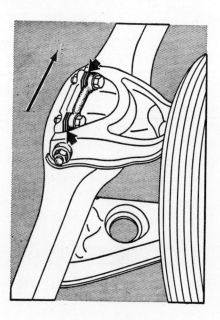

joint moves fore and aft through an arc to change caster. It is possible to change caster by removing a shim from *one* bolt without adding it to the other, but this will disturb the camber angle. Removing a shim from one side and adding it to the other does not disturb the camber angle setting. Using the example above, to change caster toward *positive*, remove a shim from the rear mounting bolt and install it at the front. To change toward *negative*, remove shim from the front mounting bolt and install it at rear.

Camber is changed by adding or subtracting an equal number of shims of equal thickness on both upper control arm mounting bolts. Using the example above, *removing* an equal number of shims from the front and rear bolts changes camber toward *negative*. *Adding* an equal number of shims changes camber toward *positive*.

Caster and camber may be adjusted together in one operation. Simply loosen the inner shaft mounting bolts, shift one shim from one bolt to the other to adjust caster. Then, remove shims from

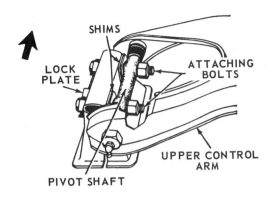

SHIMS

LOCK PLATE

ATTACHING BOLTS

UPPER CONTROL ARM

PIVOT SHAFT

Fig. 9-16. Upper control arm mounting showing location of caster and camber shims on *wheel* side of mounting bracket.

or add shims to (in equal numbers) both mounting bolts to adjust *camber.* Tighten the bolts securely and recheck gauge readings.

Not all cars have shims mounted in the manner previously illustrated in Figure 9-16 (toward the wheel). On some cars they are mounted on the inside, toward the engine. Always look at shim arrangements to determine the desired direction of change *before* loosening the bolts.

Following the illustrations (Figures 9-17 and 9-18), to change caster toward *positive*, remove a shim from the front mounting bolt and install it at the rear. To change caster toward *negative*, remove shim from the rear mounting bolt and install at the front.

To change camber toward *positive*, remove an equal number and thickness of shims from the front and rear bolts. Adding an equal number and thickness of shims changes camber toward *negative*.

ECCENTRIC ADJUSTMENTS

Before the ball joint system was adopted, virtually every car had some form of eccentric bolt or eccentric bush-

Fig. 9-17. Upper control arm mounting showing location of caster and camber shims on *engine* side of mounting bracket. (Bear Manufacturing Company)

Fig. 9-18. Caster and camber shims between upper control arm and frame brackets, *engine* side. (Bear Manufacturing Company)

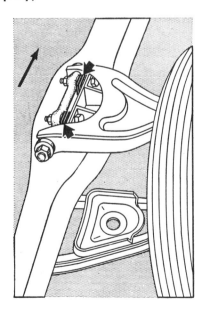

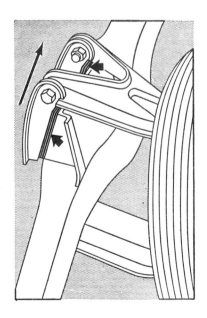

1. Lock screw.
2. Eccentric bushing.
3. Knuckle support.
4. Adjusting tool.

Fig. 9-19. Eccentric bushing adjustment on older Chrysler cars. (Bear Manufacturing Company)

Fig. 9-20. Eccentric bolt adjustment on older General Motors cars. (Bear Manufacturing Company)

ing (see Figure 9-19) in the upper end of the spindle support for adjusting caster and camber. Ford, Lincoln, and Mercury had both an eccentric bolt in the upper end of the spindle support and a threaded bolt in the lower end. The threaded bolt in the lower end controlled caster while the upper eccentric controlled camber. Adjustment of the upper eccentric bolt was obtained either by using wrenches on the hex head bolt or, on some General Motors cars, by removing the grease fitting and adjusting the eccentric bolt with an Allen wrench.

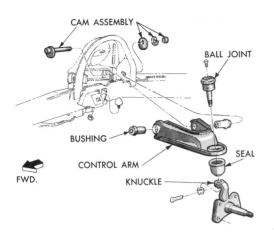

Fig. 9-21. Upper control arm mounting showing location of caster and camber cam-bolt assemblies. (Chrysler-Plymouth Division of Chrysler Corporation)

CAM-BOLT ADJUSTMENTS

Another form of eccentric adjustment, found today on Chrysler, Cadillac El-dorado, and some Rambler vehicles, is the Cam and Bolt assembly located at the inner pivot points of the upper control arms.

Caster is obtained by turning both cam bolts toward the rear of the car for *positive* direction, and toward the front for *negative* direction.

Camber is obtained from the cam-like arrangement of the assembly. As the bolts are turned, the high part of

Fig. 9-22. Upper control arm mounting showing location of caster and camber cams on Cadillac Eldorado front-wheel drive suspension. (Cadillac Motor Car Division of General Motors Corporation)

Camber and Caster Cams

the cam causes the upper control arm to move out away from the engine (positive) or in toward the engine (negative). Like shims, both cams at each pivot point must be turned together and equally.

A suggested adjustment procedure is presented below:

1. Adjust the caster angle *first*.
   a. Loosen both cam-bolt assemblies and on one cam bolt adjust one-half the amount of correction required.
   b. Adjust the remaining amount of caster on the other cam bolt assembly.
2. Adjust camber by turning both cams equally. Camber correction is obtained without disturbing caster.
3. Tighten cam-bolt assemblies securely and recheck caster and camber readings.

Fig. 9-23. Lower control arm cam-bolt assembly showing location of camber adjustment on some Rambler cars. (Bear Manufacturing Company)

Fig. 9-24. Upper control arm mounting showing location of Rambler cam-bolt assemblies for adjusting caster and camber. (Bear Manufacturing Company)

ECCENTRIC-STRUT ROD ADJUSTMENTS

Cadillac cars employ a camber eccentric at the upper ball joint for camber adjustments and an adjustable strut rod mounted between the frame and lower control arm for caster adjustments.

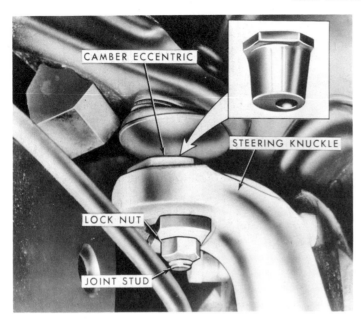

Fig. 9-25. Upper ball joint camber eccentric adjustment. (Cadillac Motor Car Division of General Motors Corporation)

Fig. 9-26. Strut rod caster adjustment. (Cadillac Motor Car Division of General Motors Corporation)

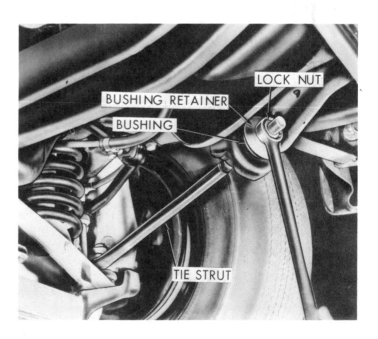

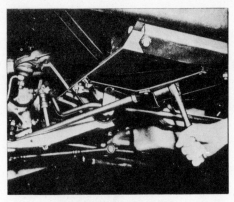

ADJUSTING CASTER

ADJUSTING CAMBER

Fig. 9-27. An adjustable strut rod and a cam-bolt assembly are provided on other cars. (Bear Manufacturing Company)

Caster is adjusted by lengthening or shortening the strut rod. Loosening the inner retaining nut and tightening the outer one causes the *lower* ball joint to move toward the front of the car (positive caster). Lengthening the strut rod moves the *lower* ball joint toward rear of car (negative caster).

Many Chevrolet cars are similar in design except that camber is adjusted by means of a cam-bolt assembly located at the inner pivot point of the lower control arm.

On those cars having the caster adjustment at the strut rod, it is generally advisable to adjust camber first, then caster.

SLIDING INNER SHAFT ADJUSTMENTS

Late model Ford and Mercury cars have elongated holes in the crossmember. Once the upper control arm inner shaft mounting bolts are loosened, a pry bar or special tool is used to shift the inner shaft to adjust the caster and camber angles.

Fig. 9-28. Upper control arm sliding inner shaft, caster and camber adjustment.

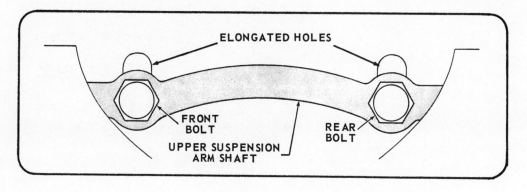

ELONGATED HOLES

FRONT BOLT

REAR BOLT

UPPER SUSPENSION ARM SHAFT

Fig. 9-29. Adjusting caster and camber with correction tool for late Ford models. (Bear Manufacturing Company)

shaft must be raised to free serrated surface from crossmember.

The special correction tool is installed against the vehicle frame siderail and connected to the upper ball joint. Then, a Holding Fixture is attached to the upper control arm inner shaft to raise the shaft from the crossmember. Once the locking bolts and shaft are free from the crossmember, caster and camber are adjusted at the correction bolts (C) of the special correction tool. Note that a positive link is maintained between the car frame and spindle support arm during the entire adjustment process.

The Ford Pinto models offer another sliding inner shaft arrangement. Two special tools (one for each end of the inner shaft) are slipped into place, with the lower stud end of the tool fitting into a hole in the frame member. The threaded bolt provides infinite caster/camber adjustment when shaft mounting bolts are loosened.

Caster is obtained by shifting one end of the inner shaft in the desired direction. *Camber* is obtained by shifting both ends of the inner shaft equally, in toward the engine (negative) or out away from the engine (positive).

Another kind of sliding inner shaft arrangement requires a special alinement correction tool. (See Figure 9-30.) Both the underside of the inner shaft and a special caged nut, located inside the front crossmember, have serrated surfaces that provide a viselike grip to the crossmember. Before the shaft can be repositioned, (1) the locking bolts must be loosened approximately 1/4" and driven downward (to free lower serrated caged nut) and (2) the inner

Fig. 9-30. A kind of upper arm, sliding inner shaft arrangement with serrations located on underside of inner shaft and caged nut. (Bear Manufacturing Company)

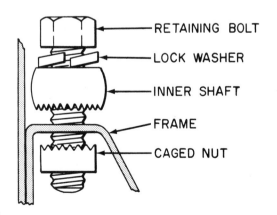

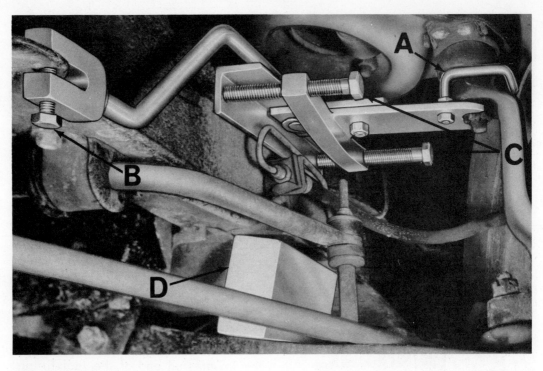

Fig. 9-31. Sliding upper inner shaft caster and camber correction tool (Ford Fairlane). (Bear Manufacturing Company)

Fig. 9-32. Sliding upper inner shaft, upper holding fixture (Ford Fairlane). (Bear Manufacturing Company)

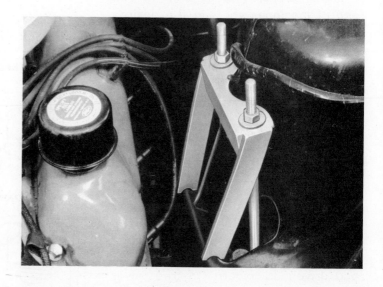

Fig. 9-33. Adjusting caster and camber with special tool for Ford Pinto Models. (Bear Manufacturing Company)

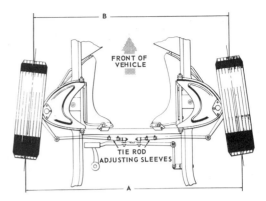

Fig. 9-34. Toe-in adjustment is made by turning the tie rod adjusting sleeves. (Bear Manufacturing Company)

After camber and caster are adjusted, all adjustment means (including cam-bolt assemblies, shim bolts, eccentrics, strut rods) must be securely tightened; the front end of the vehicle bounced up and down (at its center); and a final check made of the alinement readings. This is necessary because the correction of one angle may well have disturbed the setting of another on the same wheel. Also caster and/or camber settings may even change on the opposite wheel. Consequently, it is always good practice to recheck the settings before proceeding to the next step.

Toe-in and Steering Wheel Position Adjustment

Following the caster and camber corrections, toe-in is the last of the adjustable angles to be serviced on any vehicle. Wheel alinement angles are all closely related and affect each other. Change in caster and/or camber adjustments will affect toe-in.

Toe-in is adjusted in the same manner on all cars and trucks. There are one or more threaded sleeves on the tie rod steering linkage system that controls the length of the tie rods. Turning the right- and left-hand threaded sleeves lengthens or shortens the tie rods and changes the amount of toe-in of the front wheels.

During the correction of toe-in, it is important that the steering system be centered or the steering wheel "positioned" properly at the same time.

Proper steering wheel "position" means:

1. The steering wheel in straight ahead position.

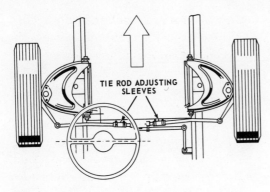

2. Steering gear on "hi-point" position.
3. Front wheels in correct toe-in setting.

Have you ever driven down the highway in a straight ahead direction and noticed the steering wheel was not centered? Do you know what is taking

Fig. 9-35. Centering steering wheel position is accomplished at the same time toe-in is adjusted. (Bear Manufacturing Company)

Fig. 9-36. One method of adjusting toe-in and centering steering wheel position involves use of the drive-over wheel alinement tester. (Bear Manufacturing Company)

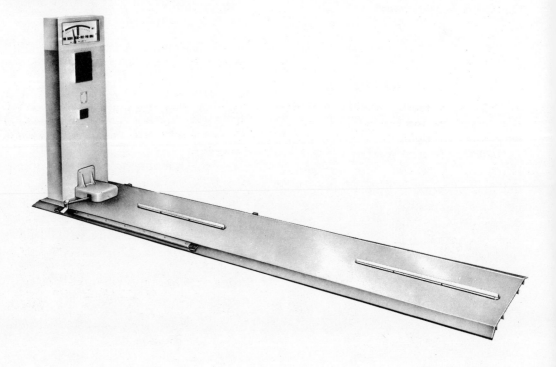

place? The car is being steered off the "hi-point" of the steering gear. The steering gear, when not centered, causes "play" in straight ahead direction and is subject to damage when the front wheels transmit road shocks through the steering linkage. Free play in the steering gear also leads to wander and weave causing poor directional control of the vehicle. Consequently, as "steering wheel position" correction relates to wheel alinement adjustment procedures, it is performed at the same time toe-in is adjusted—the final adjustment on any wheel alinement job and a most important one!

One method of making this adjustment is the use of the drive-over type of alinement tester. Drive vehicle slowly and straight across tester with hands off steering wheel. As the front wheels make full contact with each blade of the alinement tester, observe the position of the steering wheel.

If the steering wheel position is correct (straight across) but toe-in is not, it will be necessary to adjust both tie rods an equal amount. This procedure changes toe-in but leaves the steering wheel in its straight ahead position.

If the steering wheel position is not correct, the specialist can, by following the chart, correct both toe-in and steering wheel position in one operation. An easy rule to remember is to adjust the tie rod adjusting sleeves so that the front wheels are moved toward the low steering wheel spoke position (see chart). Remember that toe-in equalizes itself when the vehicle travels down the highway. Consequently, when the car is in motion, we do not have more toe-in on one wheel than on the other. When adjusting steering wheel position, then, it's a matter of positioning the front wheels for the driver to overcorrect, in a sense, to bring the steering wheel into straight ahead position.

Fig. 9-37. With steering wheel low on right side, adjust tie rod sleeves to turn front wheels toward *right*. (Bear Manufacturing Company)

Fig. 9-38. With steering wheel low on left side, adjust tie rod sleeves to turn front wheels toward *left*. (Bear Manufacturing Company)

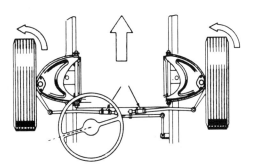

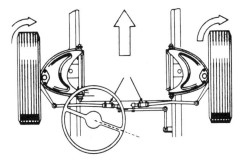

REVIEW QUIZ

The following quiz is designed to help you review the different kinds of wheel alinement adjustment provisions for caster, camber, and toe-in. Be selective in your choice of answers and check against the answer sheet at the end of this text. Only one answer is correct.

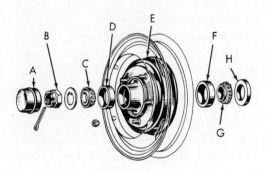

Fig. 9-39. Exploded view of front wheel bearing assemblies.

Directions: Identify the correct answer by encircling the letter corresponding to the correct component part.

1. D is the:
   - a. Outer wheel bearing.
   - b. Inner bearing cup.
   - c. Outer bearing cup.
   - d. Thrust washer.
2. H is the:
   - a. Grease retainer.
   - b. Inner wheel bearing.
   - c. Outer wheel bearing.
   - d. Inner bearing cup.
3. G is the:
   - a. Outer grease retainer.
   - b. Inner wheel bearing.
   - c. Inner bearing cup.
   - d. Grease cup.

4. The inner wheel bearing is:
   - a. Larger than the outer wheel bearing.
   - b. Smaller than the outer wheel bearing.
   - c. Same size as the outer wheel bearing.
   - d. Interchangeable with the outer wheel bearing.
5. A front wheel bearing adjustment permits:
   - a. .010" of looseness.
   - b. No looseness.
   - c. .020" of looseness.
   - d. None of these.
6. To properly aline the front wheels, corrections must be made in the following sequence: (which one is not in proper order?):
   - a. Adjust toe-in.
   - b. Adjust caster.
   - c. Adjust camber.
   - d. Adjust steering wheel position.
7. Which one of the following is not involved in caster adjustment?
   - a. Shims.
   - b. Eccentrics.
   - c. Adjusting sleeves.
   - d. Strut rods.
8. Which one of the following is not involved in camber adjustment?
   - a. Cam-bolt assembly.
   - b. Shims.
   - c. Eccentrics.
   - d. Strut rods.
9. This is a:

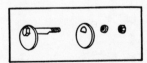

   - a. Cam-bolt assembly.
   - b. Eccentric bushing.
   - c. Eccentric bolt.
   - d. Threaded round pin.

10. Shims are used on some vehicles for:

    a. Caster correction.
    b. King pin adjustment.
    c. Tie rod adjustment.
    d. Toe-out correction.

11. Wheel alinement corrections on late model Ford cars are made by:

    a. Shim adjustment.
    b. Eccentric adjustment.
    c. Eccentric–strut rod adjustment.
    d. Sliding inner shaft adjustment.

12. Wheel alinement corrections on late model Chrysler product cars are made by:

    a. Eccentric–strut rod adjustment.
    b. Eccentric bushings.
    c. Eccentric bolts.
    d. Cam-bolt assemblies.

13. In shifting shims, the upper ball joint moved toward the rear of the car. This indicates:

    a. Positive camber.
    b. Negative caster.
    c. Positive caster.
    d. Negative camber.

14. When an equal number of shims were added to the mounting bolts, the upper ball joint was positioned further away from the engine. This indicates:

    a. Positive caster.
    b. Positive camber.
    c. Negative caster.
    d. Negative camber.

15. Correct steering wheel "position" is important because:

    a. Car will otherwise steer to one side.
    b. It provides steering stability in straight ahead direction.
    c. It hides the speedometer from driver's view.
    d. It makes it easier to set toe-in of the front wheels.

16. The steering wheel spoke is "down" on the left while traveling straight ahead and the toe-in is correct. To properly aline the steering wheel spoke, turn:

    a. The right-hand adjusting sleeve to move right front wheel *left*.
    b. Both adjusting sleeves an equal amount so that front wheels move *right*.
    c. Both adjusting sleeves an equal amount so that front wheels move *left*.
    d. None of these.

17. A sequence for performing wheel alinement service is presented below. Which operation is out of sequence?

    a. Steering and suspension parts replacements.
    b. Steering gear adjustments.
    c. Wheel bearing adjustments.
    d. Inspecting the vehicle.
    e. Front wheel alinement adjustments.

18. Wheel alinement corrections on late model Rambler cars are made by:
    a. Shims.
    b. Eccentric–strut rod adjustment means.
    c. Eccentric bushings.
    d. Cam-bolt assemblies.

19. Turning the adjusting sleeves corrects:
    a. Toe-out on turns.
    b. Toe-change.
    c. Toe-in.
    d. None of these.

20. The caster and camber settings given in a specification chart for a particular year and model car:
    a. Must be followed exactly and no change made in them.
    b. Have been suggested by the car manufacturer as the ideal settings which will cover all operating conditions.
    c. Should be reduced by 1/2° in the negative direction if the vehicle is operated almost exclusively on sand or gravel roads.
    d. Can be varied by 1/2° plus or minus if the specifications show only one setting.

Chapter 10
ROAD TESTING AND
TROUBLE SHOOTING

Upon completion of wheel alinement services, it is recommended procedure to road test the car thoroughly to be certain (1) that customer complaints have been corrected and (2) that the vehicle has good steering response and steering stability.

ROAD TEST PROCEDURE

1. Within the first two blocks, on a level road, check vehicle for pulling to one side and the steering wheel for straight ahead position. Should car pull to one side, it may be caused by:

   a. Unequal camber between the two front wheels. Generally, a camber setting of 1/2° greater on one side will cause a car to pull.

   b. Unequal caster or an incorrect caster spread between the two front wheels.
   c. Scuffed tires or one front tire worn more than the other.
   d. Unequal air pressures.
   e. Bent or misalined suspension parts or frame misalinement.

   Should steering wheel not be in straight ahead position when traveling in straight ahead direction, it must be recentered by readjusting the tie rod adjusting sleeves. Be certain that toe-in is correct following the recentering operation.

2. If vehicle pulls to one side, correct it before completing road test.

Fig. 10-1. Driving vehicle across the wheel alinement tester to final-check the toe-in setting following the road test. (Bear Manufacturing Company)

3. At 45 mph, on hard-surfaced road, check vehicle for steering stability and wander. Turn steering wheel first in one direction, then the other, to check steering response. Response should be positive without excessive play or binding. Little effort should be needed to control vehicle direction. Any tendencies of the vehicle to move off in either direction without the driver's turning the steering wheel indicates:

    a. Steering linkage looseness.
    b. Steering gear looseness.
    c. Loosely adjusted front wheel bearings.
    d. Worn or smooth tires.

    Binding or an overtight steering response is an indication of:

    a. Incorrectly adjusted steering gear (too tight).
    b. Lack of lubrication of steering and/or suspension parts.
    c. Improperly installed idler arm or idler arm kit.
    d. Low air pressures.

4. At higher speeds check for front wheel shimmy, indicated by a rapid and sometimes violent back-and-forth shake of the steering wheel. Generally, this is caused by unbalanced front wheels and/or badly bent wheels—wheels having run-out in excess of 1/8".

5. At higher speeds, also, check for high-speed vibrations, which may be caused by:

    a. Unbalanced wheel assemblies, front and rear.
    b. Out-of-round wheels, brake drums, or tires.
    c. Cuppy tread wear on the tires.
    d. Dead or weak shock absorbers.
    e. Unbalanced or misalined drive shaft.
    f. Defective motor mounts.

6. If the vehicle steers and handles well and the steering wheel is in straight ahead position, recheck the toe-in across an Alinement Tester as a final check. Correct, if necessary.

TROUBLE SHOOTING CHART FOR WHEEL AND STEERING ALINEMENT

Hard Steering (Indicated by Tightness in Steering System)

Tire pressure low or uneven.
    Inflate tires to proper pressure.

Steering gear or connections adjusted too tightly.
    Inspect steering system for binding with front wheels off floor. Adjust as necessary and lubricate.

Steering gear, king pins, ball joints, or tie rod ends dry.
    Insufficient or incorrect lubricant. Lubricate suspension and steering linkage as required.

Caster excessive.
    Check caster and adjust.

Steering knuckle or spindle bent.
    Replace with new parts.

King pin thrust bearings worn.
    Install new bearings.

Suspension arms bent or twisted.
    Check wheel alinement angles; camber, caster, and steering axis inclination. Install new suspension arms.

Front springs sagged.
    Check vehicle spring height.

Sagged springs should be replaced with new ones. Always replace in pairs.

Frame misalined or broken.
Check car tracking and frame alinement. Correct and repair frame.

Excessive Play or Looseness in Steering System

King pins and bushings or ball joints worn.
Install new king pins and bushings or new ball joints.

Front wheel bearings incorrectly adjusted or worn.
Adjust bearings or replace with new parts.

Steering gear adjusted too loosely or worn.
Adjust or install new parts.

Steering gear mountings loose.
Tighten steering gear to frame.

Pitman arm loose on cross shaft.
Replace parts or tighten cross shaft nut.

Drag link too loose.
Adjust or replace with new parts.

Tie rod ends worn.
Install new tie rod ends.

Idler arm worn.
Install new idler arm or idler arm kit.

Erratic Steering on Application of Brakes

Tire pressure low or uneven.
Inflate tires to proper pressure.

Brakes incorrectly or unevenly adjusted.
Adjust brakes.

Brake lining oil or grease soaked.
Replace brake lining and clean brake drum.

Front wheel bearings incorrectly adjusted or worn.
Adjust bearings or replace with new parts.

Front springs and/or shock absorbers weak.
Replace with new springs and/or shock absorbers of correct type.

Caster excessive.
Check caster and adjust.

Steering knuckle or spindle bent.
Replace with new parts.

Spring "U" bolts broken or loose.
Replace or retighten.

Spring center bolt broken.
Install new center bolt.

Strut rod(s) loose.
Replace strut rod bushings.

Pulls to One Side

Tire pressures low or uneven.
Inflate tires to proper pressure.

Caster incorrect or uneven.
Check caster and adjust.

Camber excessively unequal.
Adjust camber.

Front tires scuffed.
Rotate tires.

Steering knuckle or spindle bent.
Replace with new knuckle or spindle.

Spindle support arm bent.
Replace with new arm.

Front springs sagged.
Check vehicle spring height.

Sagged springs should be replaced with new ones. Always replace in pairs.

Rear axle shifted.
Check for loose spring clips or broken center bolt. Measure from spring bolts (anchor end) to rear housing. This distance should be uniform on both sides of car.

Front suspension assembly back.
Replace parts or pull suspension assembly.

Frame misalined or broken.
Check car tracking and frame alinement. Correct and repair frame.

Scuffed Tires

Tires improperly inflated.
Inflate tires to proper pressure.

Toe-in or toe-out incorrect.
Adjust tie rods to make front wheels toe-in proper amount.

Wheels or tires out of true.
Check for wheel and tire wobble. Replace wheels or tires if necessary.

Toe-out on turns incorrect.
Install new steering arms.

Front wheel bearings incorrectly adjusted or worn.
Adjust bearings or replace with new parts.

Suspension arms bent or twisted.
Check wheel alinement angles; camber, caster, and steering axis inclination. Install new suspension arms.

Steering knuckle or spindle bent.
Replace with new parts.

Excessive speeds on turns.
Caution driver.

Cupped Tires

Tires improperly inflated.
Inflate tires to proper pressure.

Wheels, tires, or brake drums out of balance.
Balance wheels and tires. Check for eccentric brake drums, wheels, and tires and replace as necessary.

Dragging brakes (incorrectly adjusted).
Adjust brakes.

Front wheel bearings incorrectly adjusted or worn.
Adjust bearings or replace with new parts.

Camber adjustment improper.
Check camber and adjust.

Steering knuckle or spindle bent.
Replace with new knuckle or spindle.

Steering gear tie rod ends, drag link, king pins, or ball joints worn or loose.
Replace worn or loose suspension and steering parts.

Front Wheel Shimmy

Tire pressure low or uneven.
Inflate tires to proper pressure.

Steering connections incorrectly adjusted or worn.
Adjust or install new parts.

Steering gear mountings loose.
Tighten steering gear to frame.

Steering gear incorrectly adjusted.
Adjust steering gear.

Front wheel bearings incorrectly adjusted or worn.
Adjust bearings or replace with new parts.

Wheels, tires, or brake drums out of balance.

> Balance wheels and tires. Check for eccentric brake drums, wheels, and tires and replace as necessary.

Wheels or tires out of true.

> Check for wheel and tire wobble. Replace wheels or tires if necessary.

Caster incorrect or uneven.

> Check caster and adjust.

Shock absorbers dead or weak.

> Install new shock absorbers of correct type. Always replace in pairs.

A Tendency to Wander

Tire pressure low or uneven.

> Inflate tires to proper pressure.

Steering gear or connections adjusted too loosely or worn.

> Adjust or install new parts as necessary.

Steering gear or connections adjusted too tightly.

> Test steering system for binding with front wheels off floor. Adjust as necessary and lubricate.

Wheels toe-in too much or toe-out in straight-ahead position.

> Adjust tie rods to make front wheels toe-in proper amount.

Steering gear mountings loose.

> Tighten steering gear to frame.

Front wheel bearings incorrectly adjusted or worn.

> Adjust or install new bearings.

Caster incorrect.

> Check caster, adjust as necessary.

Steering knuckle bent.

> Replace with new knuckle.

Rear axle shifted (spring clip bolts loose or center bolt sheared).

> Check spring clips for looseness. Also measure from rear spring bolt to housing. This distance should be uniform on both sides of car.

Stabilizer inoperative.

> Inspect bearings and links, replacing worn parts.

Worn tires and/or smooth tread on front wheels.

> Change tires, placing those with best tread on front, or replace tires.

Road Shocks

Tire pressure low.

> Inflate tires to proper pressure.

Steering gear or connections incorrectly adjusted.

> Adjust steering gear and connections.

Caster excessive (Neg. or Pos.)

> Check caster and adjust.

Shock absorbers dead or weak.

> Install new shock absorbers of correct type. Always replace in pairs.

Front springs weak or sagged.

> Replace weak or sagged springs with new ones of correct type.

Tires of wrong type or size.

> Install new tires of correct type and size.

REVIEW QUIZ

The following quiz is designed to help you review your understanding of wheel alinement problems and their possible solutions. Choose the answer that most closely fits the problem or correction and check against the answer sheet at the end of the text. Only one answer is correct.

1. Hard steering may be caused by:
   a. Wheel bearings improperly adjusted.
   b. Worn ball joints.
   c. Dragging brakes.
   d. Lack of lubrication of tie rod ends, ball joints, or king pins, etc.

2. One of the first steps in wheel alinement is to adjust the steering gear:
   a. To correct camber misalinement.
   b. To correct toe-in misalinement.
   c. To correct caster misalinement.
   d. For proper vehicle control.

3. Excessive play or looseness in the steering system may be caused by:
   a. Loose steering gear mountings.
   b. Loose shock absorber mountings.
   c. Loose spring mountings.
   d. Overly lubricated idler arm.

4. A vehicle may pull to one side because of:
   a. Uneven tire pressures.
   b. Front wheel bearings incorrectly adjusted.
   c. Bent steering arm.
   d. A loose drag link.

5. Cuppy tire wear is a direct result of:
   a. Incorrect toe-in.
   b. Worn steering and suspension parts.
   c. Shifted rear axle.
   d. Incorrect caster.

6. A vehicle may pull to one side because of:
   a. A worn, scuffed tire.
   b. Equal camber.
   c. Grease soaked brake lining.
   d. Loose steering gear mountings.

7. A tire may wear on one side only because of:
   a. Unequal caster.
   b. Incorrect steering axis inclination.
   c. Incorrect toe-in.
   d. Road crown.

8. Road shock may be caused by:
   a. Dry steering gear.
   b. High air pressure in tires.
   c. Weak shock absorbers.
   d. Bent tie rod.

9. A vehicle that has a tendency to wander may have:
   a. Worn idler arm.
   b. Worn steering arm.
   c. Worn pitman arm.
   d. Bent tie rod.

10. A steering gear adjusted too tightly may cause:
    a. A pull to one side.
    b. Wander.
    c. Road shock.
    d. Erratic steering on application of brakes.

11. A tire showing underinflation wear will have:
    a. One side of the tire tread worn.
    b. Spotty wear on one side of tread.
    c. Both sides of tire tread worn.
    d. Center of tire tread worn.

12. Front wheel shimmy may be caused by:
    a. Bent spindle support arm.
    b. Negative caster.
    c. Unbalanced wheels.
    d. None of these.

13. Better tread on rear tires than on front ones may cause:
    a. Front wheel shimmy.
    b. Pull to one side.
    c. Wander.
    d. Misalinement.

14. A pitted front wheel bearing will cause:
    a. Cuppy tire wear.
    b. Vehicle to wander.
    c. Vehicle to pull to one side.
    d. Unbalanced wheel.

15. The purpose of road testing a vehicle upon completion of work done is to check against original customer complaints. Which one of the following does not belong in the road test?
    a. Pull to one side.
    b. Wander and weave.
    c. Wheel shimmy.
    d. Tire wear.
    e. Road shock and vibrations.

16. The final adjustment or check before returning car to owner, following the road test, is:
    a. To adjust steering gear.
    b. To adjust front wheel bearings.
    c. To drive across alinement tester and correct toe-in.
    d. To lubricate all front end parts.

17. Power steering gears have a tendency to cover up:
    a. Pull to one side.
    b. Wander and weave.
    c. Erratic steering.
    d. Hard steering.

18. On a front tire, the presence of a feather edge on the tire tread ribs toward the center of the vehicle indicates:
    a. Excessive caster.
    b. Insufficient toe-in.
    c. Tight front wheel bearings.
    d. Too much toe-in.

19. The most likely cause of wheel tramp or high speed vibration is:
    a. Loose steering gear mountings.
    b. Loose strut rod.
    c. Improper tire pressure.
    d. Improper balance of wheels and tires.

20. Tire wear is not caused by:
    a. Excessive toe-in.
    b. Excessive toe-out.
    c. Excessive camber.
    d. Caster angle set incorrectly.

INDEX

ANSWERS TO QUIZZES

CHAPTER 1
FRONT SUSPENSION DESIGNS

quiz answer sheet

1.	c.	11.	c.
2.	a.	12.	d.
3.	b.	13.	a.
4.	c.	14.	d.
5.	b.	15.	a.
6.	b.	16.	b.
7.	c.	17.	d.
8.	d.	18.	b.
9.	c.	19.	a.
10.	c.	20.	a.

CHAPTER 2
INSPECTING THE VEHICLE

quiz answer sheet

1.	b.	11.	c.
2.	a.	12.	c.
3.	a.	13.	b.
4.	d.	14.	d.
5.	a.	15.	d.
6.	d.	16.	c.
7.	a.	17.	d.
8.	c.	18.	b.
9.	a.	19.	c.
10.	b.	20.	b.

CHAPTER 3
STEERING GEAR SERVICES

quiz answer sheet

1. d.   11. a.
2. b.   12. c.
3. a.   13. c.
4. c.   14. c.
5. a.   15. a.
6. c.   16. b.
7. b.   17. a.
8. d.   18. d.
9. c.   19. d.
10. b.   20. c.

CHAPTER 4
WHEEL BALANCING SERVICES

quiz answer sheet

1. a.   6. b.
2. c.   7. c.
3. c.   8. b.
4. e.   9. a.
5. b.   10. d.

CHAPTER 5
WHEEL ALINEMENT ANGLES —CASTER

quiz answer sheet

1.	*f.*	11.	*a.*
2.	*d.*	12.	*c.*
3.	*b.*	13.	*c.*
4.	*d.*	14.	*c.*
5.	*a.*	15.	*c.*
6.	*c.*	16.	*c.*
7.	*d.*	17.	*b.*
8.	*b.*	18.	*d.*
9.	*d.*	19.	*c.*
10.	*c.*	20.	*a.*

CHAPTER 6
WHEEL ALINEMENT ANGLES —CAMBER

quiz answer sheet

1.	*d.*	11.	*c.*
2.	*a.*	12.	*b.*
3.	*b.*	13.	*c.*
4.	*c.*	14.	*d.*
5.	*d.*	15.	*a.*
6.	*b.*	16.	*c.*
7.	*c.*	17.	*c.*
8.	*c.*	18.	*c.*
9.	*a.*	19.	*d.*
10.	*b.*	20.	*b.*

CHAPTER 7
WHEEL ALINEMENT ANGLES —STEERING AXIS INCLINATION AND TURNING RADIUS

quiz answer sheet

1.	c.	11.	c.
2.	c.	12.	c.
3.	a.	13.	d.
4.	c.	14.	d.
5.	c.	15.	a.
6.	b.	16.	d.
7.	c.	17.	c.
8.	c.	18.	a.
9.	d.	19.	c.
10.	b.	20.	d.

CHAPTER 8
WHEEL ALINEMENT ANGLES—TOE-IN

quiz answer sheet

1.	b.	11.	b.
2.	c.	12.	c.
3.	b.	13.	a.
4.	d.	14.	b.
5.	a.	15.	c.
6.	a.	16.	b.
7.	c.	17.	c.
8.	b.	18.	c.
9.	d.	19.	d.
10.	d.	20.	b.

CHAPTER 9
WHEEL ALINEMENT CORRECTIONS

quiz answer sheet

1.	c.	11.	d.
2.	a.	12.	d.
3.	b.	13.	c.
4.	a.	14.	b.
5.	b.	15.	b.
6.	a.	16.	c.
7.	c.	17.	d.
8.	d.	18.	d.
9.	a.	19.	c.
10.	a.	20.	b.

CHAPTER 10
ROAD TESTING AND TROUBLE SHOOTING

quiz answer sheet

1.	d.	11.	c.
2.	d.	12.	c.
3.	a.	13.	c.
4.	a.	14.	a.
5.	b.	15.	d.
6.	a.	16.	c.
7.	c.	17.	d.
8.	c.	18.	d.
9.	a.	19.	d.
10.	b.	20.	d.

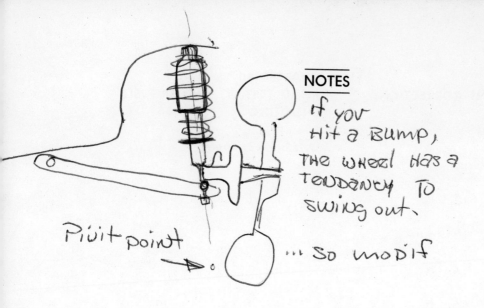

If you Hit a Bump, the wheel Has a Tendency To swing out.

... So modif

Pivit point →◁.

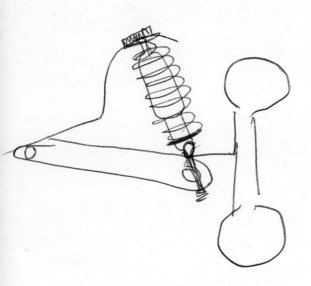

NOTES

NOTES

NOTES

NOTES

NOTES

NOTES